CW01500308

P er the official results and my maths, my 2021 Tour de France had lasted 315,130 seconds and I wouldn't have changed any of them, except the last 30. For over a century of the world's greatest bike race, sport's most gruelling odyssey, riders had crossed the finish line in Paris and tasted a blissful relief from the back of their throat to the tip of every nerve. In most cases they had merely survived to tell the tale, whereas over the last three weeks I'd rewritten the Tour's history books. Put my name to what some hyperbolically inclined pundits had already called 'the greatest comeback ever'. In cycling or any other sport.

And yet instead of relief, all I could feel was regret. A desperate desire to go back. Erase and rewind – like the title of a famous song. Rescript those last ten seconds. Reshoot the whole ending.

Because that's also what it could have been: the end. Roll credits. Mic drop. I'd thought about it. Ever since I'd equalled the great Eddy Merckx's record of 34 Tour de France stage wins in Carcassonne a week earlier, the idea had been there – a little voice in the back of my head, maybe no more than a whisper, consistent but not insistent, telling me that this would be the ultimate exclamation mark. Arms aloft, the Arc de Triomphe in my eyeline, the setting sun painting Paris gold, the win counter stopped and deactivated on 35 …

Perfection. An apotheosis. An ending that not Hollywood, not AI, not Renoir or Monet or Van Gogh could have programmed, dreamed up or drawn.

One fraction of a second within those 30, one decision, had ruined it all. As we swung around and off the Place de la Concorde, with the road bending to the right, I'd seen Wout van Aert move onto and past my left shoulder, then followed my instinct and his wheel, not that of my faithful lead-out man Michael Mørkøv. In sprinting, one mistake isn't fatal on its own but, the closer you get to the finish line, the more errors tend to compound in an accelerating, inescapable spiral of doom. In this case, within a few seconds, I was wedged between Van Aert's back wheel, another Belgian rider, Jonas Rickaert, and the crash barriers, and there was simply nowhere to move. Checkmate. Fucked. To quote another pop song, so much for my happy ending.

The last day of the Tour is always a strange and tense one in the sense that what is often described as a formality, a procession for 95 per cent of the peloton, is anything but for a sprinter. The final bunch gallop of the Tour has often been referred to as 'the sprinters' world championship', with all the accompanying prestige but also pressure. The stakes were sky-high … and here, for me, stratospheric, with the Merckx record, what I'd already achieved in this Tour, and also, yes, speculation in the media about whether a win would see me ride off into the sunset.

Now, in an instant, all of the suspense and excitement had been sucked from the air. I'd 'lost', and the juxtaposition of the demob-happiness that reigned around me and my disappointment had a jarring effect on anyone and everyone who caught my eye. How could they or I reconcile the miracle of the last three weeks – a Tour in which I'd confounded every critic, every precedent, every expectation after three winless years of illness, doubt and even humiliation – with this resounding anticlimax?

Sheepish smiles everywhere. Pats on the back and the shoulder. A confetti shower of blandishments. Words like 'anyway', 'still', 'nevertheless'. Reminders that those 30 seconds, what had just happened, didn't change or take away anything from the previous three weeks. I was still in green. That the record was mine and Merckx's. A thirty-fifth would have been a bonus, the cherry on the icing on the cake.

Soon enough, I was in Peta's arms. Usually seeing her and the kids could salve any wound inflicted in a race, real or metaphorical. And yet I couldn't snap out of my daze, couldn't shake the obsession. Redact those 30 seconds. Erase and rewind.

Would I have actually quit? Hard to know for sure but I had genuinely, if not extensively, thought about it. Part of me wonders now whether, in the euphoria, instinct or impulse would have taken over and I'd just have blurted it: 'I always wanted to go out at the top and it can't get any better than this ...'

One thing I can say with four years' hindsight: I'm pretty sure I would have regretted calling it quits then and there. We've all heard it a million times – that an athlete wants to 'go out on their own terms' or 'go out at the top'. But anyone who's sought and taken the advice of former professional sportsmen or -women knows that there's another, more realistic and important principal to abide by: that you should never say goodbye without knowing exactly what's coming next. Preferably, in fact, that new life, job and to a certain extent identity would be not only known but prepared, curated, sitting and waiting for you. I actually did already have a plan for 2022; I'd negotiated its finer details just a few weeks before the Tour – and it was to remain a professional bike rider in my current team.

To this I'd added my own golden rule, again based on the counsel of former colleagues: never make the decision after a bad day on the bike when some sort of pain might impair your judgement, be it physical pain after slogging over some hideous alpine pass, or mental having just suffered a major set-back like the one I'd just experienced.

In short, rationality should always prevail over emotion … but that was a tough battle to adjudicate at the end of a Tour de France, particularly one as relentlessly emotional as this. Looking back now, I can say that, in this case, defeat and regret were at least better instructors than triumph and elation. Maybe no amount of careful reasoning could have doused those emotions and the temptation to make a grand, dramatic gesture and life-changing pronouncement. The heart, in those charged moments, has its own compelling language.

Erase and rewind, no, but I could run another tape.

Above all, if there was any clarity in those instants and the hours that followed it was in my conviction that, at 36, I had more to give. I'd started the season hopeful that I would prove myself after three years in the doldrums. Slowly at first, that hope had hardened into something resembling confidence, and later cast-iron certainty when I won four stages at the Tour of Turkey in April. Races were getting faster, riders stronger, sports science had changed the game, and yet my numbers said that I was better even than I had been in my mid-twenties, back when I could barely lose. Not only that but it was easy to see where I could make even more gains in 2022. In my best seasons, I'd focused all of my planning, all of my training, every race in the first six months of the year on being in peak fitness for the Tour. Here I'd received my summons with … a week's notice. I didn't need to strain or squint very hard to imagine myself in August 2021, newly retired, Merckx's record not only equalled but eclipsed, sat on a couch or sun lounger, haunted by the knowledge that I'd left more wins and more unexplored potential on the table. When I pictured that version of myself, I didn't visualise a fully accomplished, contented man. He was certainly not a happier 36-year-old than the one I'd been over the previous three weeks or even few months.

Mainly for this reason – more than any symbolism or personal sense of completing some sort of abstract narrative arc – quitting would have been a mistake. With time, I suppose you could even say I'd be almost grateful for that fateful half-minute. The questions about whether I'd even get picked for the 2022 Tour de France would come later; for now, there was a sense that what had occurred over the previous weeks had been some kind of once-in-eternity communion of the gods and cosmic forces, a freak atom-splitting occurrence, a gift sent my way once that could never be repeated. If I'd looked hard, I'd have seen it in the faces of some, if not all, who offered their commiserative congratulations – or congratulatory commiserations – behind the podium. They probably imagined me coming back year after year, a cautionary tale of physical decay and mental delusion egging each other on. I wouldn't have been the first or last, they'd think – the umpteenth victim of 'one-last-fight syndrome'. 'If only he'd known when enough was enough.'

For a few years now the last stage of the Tour has finished in the early evening, in the 'golden hour', so to speak. For TV it means a nicer light, better pictures, Paris looking even more beautiful, whereas for us riders it meant crossing the line in near darkness and celebration dinners that stretched deep into the early hours. Ours that year was nothing raucous – a nice dinner back at the team hotel, with riders, staff and families. One of the highlights was a video put together by our team press officer, Phil Lowe, who'd vox-popped various people about my Tour and whole career. In the clip, Brian Holm, one of my best mates and longest-serving directeurs, described the whole saga as being 'like a Hitchcock movie with a twist of *Fawlty Towers*', which I thought was pretty accurate and amusing. There were messages from Dave Brailsford, who called me 'the greatest of all time', the England footballer Jordan Henderson and the England football manager Gareth Southgate. The video ended with Peta talking about how she and we as a family had worked so hard for me to experience success at the Tour one more time, as a sort of reverence to my love for the race.

One more time or one last time? She hadn't known and neither had I.

What I also didn't know that night was how much that damned last half-minute of the 2021 Tour would be seized upon, obsessed over and spun into a storyline in which I was the unwitting and unwilling central character. One thing about that Tour – the prelude, the three weeks themselves and the postscript – remains soldered into my memory: my target, my holy grail, had always been 'the Merckx record', 34 stage victories – four more than when I started the 2021 Tour. Not 'one more than Merckx'. Not 35. That number had not been remotely on my radar. My first words when I reached the mark were to my team-mate Davide Ballerini, whose face was the first that I saw in the finish line melee in Carcassonne. *'Abbiamo fatto la storia –* we've made history!' In the minutes, hours and days that followed, though, I could tell from the journalists' questions that the goalpost-removal company was already hard at work. For them, suddenly, 'the Merckx record' meant 35 and not 34, i.e. going past and not equalling the G.O.A.T. I desperately wanted to win in Paris because it was Paris and because I desperately wanted to win every sprint at the Tour de France; not, contrary to what those pundits, some keyboard warriors and remote-control experts wanted to believe, because my lifetime's quest or crusade was somehow still incomplete.

Again, I could never have anticipated that night in Paris or even over the next few weeks that this would be the mood music, the soundtrack to the rest of my career. A broken record that, every time I heard it, made me wince or bristle. I'm self-critical enough to acknowledge the chip on the shoulder that others have often said is my most potent mental weapon. Sometimes you'll even hear me call it by its name: 'That was my Chip talking ...' I'll say, or 'I could have let it go, but my Chip …' I don't deny it. Maybe my Chip was why '35' became such a sensitive subject … or maybe I was also perfectly entitled to resent the constant interrogation or even just a *feeling* that that question loomed over everything: *Yeah, that's cool … but when are you going to win 35?* I could see it in people's eyes, *hear it* in their internal monologue. This when, rationally, mathematically, in the history books and in my own head, I ALREADY HAD THE RECORD. *With Eddy Merckx*. Fact. Over. End of story. At least to me …

And, again, here I'm going to try and be self-aware. Because in the same way that I can admit the chip on my shoulder is real, I also know from experience that I can, ahem, struggle with what here I'll just call 'inflexible thinking'. It'll come up again, so we can leave the self-diagnosis and Freudian hypotheses until later in the book, but suffice it to say that the '35 question' was a good and long-running example of me simply not being able to comprehend – let alone indulge – a prevailing thought process. Was that because, actually, this vicarious need there seemed be for a thirty-fifth victory put me under pressure? Was that it? The intolerable echo of an internal, subconscious bully in my own head, who wouldn't leave me be until, after the victory lap, I'd also got up on stage for a virtuoso encore? Was I blinded by indignation – that, after everything I'd given and won, 'they' were still baying for me to prove myself and ready to strike me down if I didn't deliver?

Whatever it was, over the next three years I would have to grit my teeth and bear this cross. Meanwhile, I'd be fighting a simultaneous battle against something much less abstract – the relentless onward march of time. I'd celebrated my thirty-sixth birthday in the May before the Tour, and the history books made grim reading: only 16 riders in the 118-year history of the Tour had won stages at a more advanced age than I was in Carcassonne. Of these, only one, the Italian Alessandro Petacchi, was a sprinter. And it got worse: not a single rider this century had done it after turning 37, as I would the following May.

There were also some silver linings. Causes for comfort, some of them genuine, sturdy, backed by evidence, others a bit more speculative. The fact that I could both feel and see in the data that I was improving was one reason to be optimistic. Another was that, to put it bluntly, you wouldn't have found any precedents for a lot of what I'd achieved in my career. Sprinters before me who had won 34 Tour stages? Of course, zero. But also: no other sprinter had won Tour stages 13 years apart. As much as I'd routinely downplayed my talent throughout my career, I couldn't deny what the bare statistics clearly stated – that I was unique. Be it because of my genetic wiring, hard work, chip on the shoulder – whatever the explanation. And unique was presumably what I'd continue to be.

Other, more fanciful supporting evidence for my continued longevity included the 'miles on the clock' theory.

The idea that the seasons 2018 to 2020 hadn't 'counted' in terms of wear and tear, physical or mental, because of the Epstein–Barr virus that had cut me off at the waist, in racing terms. I went three years without racing one of the three-week Grand Tours – the Giro d'Italia, Tour de France and Vuelta a España. Hence, you could make the argument – and some, including my coach, Vasilis Anastopoulos, did – that I was three years younger than my passport suggested in 'cyclist years'. There was no science to back the notion up, but if someone else was going to hand me the keys to some age-defying time machine, it wasn't going to be me checking under the bonnet.

So, overall, I could be hopeful … but, equally, I knew that, for me as well, the years would keep slipping through my clenched fists. I'd had my first daughter, Delilah, at 26 and two sons since then. The kids and fatherhood had completely changed my relationship with time, parallel to the natural shifts in perspective that we all undergo as we age. My first son, Frey, was born in 2015 and my second, Casper, in 2018, and over the next two years I was away maybe more than ever, training and desperately straining to get back to my best level. Then Covid came and suddenly I'd never spent so much time at home – and I loved it. Those few months of total lockdown in 2020, in particular, were absolutely precious, like some kind of delayed windfall on all my absences over the previous few years. Had the 2021 Tour been my farewell, this could also have been my new reality ... and, yet once again, by carrying on, I was also extending that old, familiar deal with the Devil. Another year, at least, of Peta doing the work of two parents. Another year of guilt. Another year of missed birthdays, other landmarks and the small, spontaneous pleasures that come with being there, immersed in their lives, every single day.

In part, I was carrying on for them and their futures, but mainly I was carrying on for myself. Because I wasn't done. I'd been a competitive cyclist for over two decades, yet the main fuel, the passion that had fired me throughout that time still burned. I wasn't weary or bored or aware of any work in the world that could give me sensations like the ones I experienced in the saddle, winning bike races. I still adored it. One thing that had changed and grown over the years was also my appreciation of that passion, my gratitude – an acknowledgement of how rare it was to be blessed with such a thing. And of the duty to honour it. Not just cast that passion away before it had exhaled its final breath. This was something that having kids and watching them discover their own interests had also helped me to grasp. Whatever role it had played in my career, the victories and the laurels, my passion was precious and mine to cherish, just as I always had. That meant no one beyond the moated wall of my own family had any right whatsoever to suggest or imply that it was time to give it up and move on. Because, actually, every sacrifice that Peta and the kids had made over the previous few years had been for this purpose: to allow me to keep following my passion. Discarding or dishonouring it before the expiry date would also be dishonouring them.

So on I would ride. To what destination – thirty-fifth stage win or many more, or not even another appearance at the Tour – I didn't know. But I had an inkling and, deep down, a confidence that those 30 seconds would not define my Tour de France career.

CHAPTER 1

At the beginning of the 2021 Tour there had been no foretaste or hint of any of this. 'The greatest come-back in sport', as *GQ* dubbed it later, had actually begun at the Tour of Turkey in the April, with my four stage wins there. At that point it had still looked unfathomable that I'd be picked for the Tour, given that the team had the standout sprinter from the previous year's edition, Sam Bennett, in its ranks and because I hadn't won anything – not even a village kermesse or 'fairground race' for three years. Sam, though, struggled with knee injuries through the late spring, while I went to the Tour of Belgium and won again. It was also there, before I even knew that I'd be going to the Tour de France and effectively taking Sam's place, that my Deceuninck–QuickStep team manager Patrick Lefevere had started talking to me about 2022.

It was a typical Patrick negotiation: posh restaurant, good wine, plenty of laughs and then, finally, an hour or so in, him matter-of-factly leaning forward and naming your six-figure price – or rather his – in the same tone that a minute ago he'd asked whether they had a different vintage of the Château Cheval Blanc. He said his number, I said mine and, after a bit of back forth, we finally settled on €500,000 plus bonuses. It wasn't my first negotiation with Patrick, it wouldn't be the last, and whenever we did talk money, I'd be smiling to myself at the memory of what he'd once said in an interview when I was at Dimension Data: that teams would always have to pay a premium to sign me, just because of my past achievements, status within the sport and, well, my name. It was funny to me how this 'rule' didn't seem to apply when it was him and his team negotiating with me. 'Your image in London is different from your image in West Flanders, with all due respect,' he once told me. Which may have been true … but it didn't quite square with what he'd said a few years earlier.

I didn't hold it against him. Patrick is a wily old wolf. A businessman but also a patriarch – and one whose loyalty, he often said, lay with his backroom staff more than riders – which is understandable in a sport of brief careers and short contracts. *Fair fucks*, I always thought; that philosophy partly explained a) why his team had survived for decades and b) why they had been so successful.

So, yes, by now, I knew Patrick's modus operandi, how he would play his hand and how I had to play mine. I went away that night thinking that, six months after coming to him grovelling for a contract, at least now I'd secured my future for another year and regained both a sense of agency and dignity. There were still riders in the WorldTour, even in this very team, earning double, triple what I would, with a quarter of the pedigree and a fraction of my marketability, be it in London or West Flanders. But that was a battle I no longer had the appetite for fighting. We didn't sign but another Patrick maxim went that his handshake was as good as his word.

Again, fair fucks.

Then had come the Tour. Bennett getting injured, my last-minute call-up, the greatest comeback and all that. But the Tour had started with another 'deal' with Patrick – this one entirely at his instigation on the eve of the race. We were starting in Brittany; the race was rolling out the next day and I was in my room, about to nod off when my phone rang and it was Patrick, urging me to come back down to the lobby. He'd been at dinner with his team co-owner, the Czech billionaire, Zdeněk Bakala. Evidently Bakala had been in a generous mood, because Patrick said he had a proposition for me: a nice €50,000 bonus for starting the Tour, €75,000 for any stage win, and a €15,000 for each week of the three that I completed.

It feels vulgar to mention the numbers, but I think here I need to provide some insight into how these things work in cycling, or at least how they did with me. It might also put into perspective how much stress I brought upon myself over the years by negotiating most of my own deals with teams, parallel to the endorsements and commercial stuff that I've paid managers to find and manage. Here the time-line – and therefore also the figures – are important just to understand how, a few months down the line, I was sitting across a restaurant table from Patrick again, trying not to lose my temper, in an argument about money that somehow, yet again, put my future as a rider in jeopardy.

Again, we have to go back to the Tour of Turkey in the April. As I've already mentioned, my first stage win there was also my first of any description for over three years, so a fairy tale in itself. Patrick recognised this and wanted to reward me, but of course he'd been telling me for months that he had no budget, so he called up the team bike sponsor, Specialized, and their founder, Mike Sinyard. I'd called Mike the previous autumn, with the question of whether he'd pay my mini-mum-wage salary. He'd said he wouldn't but that he *would* pay me bonuses if I won. Patrick later told me the conversation went as follows: Mike saying that it was only a stage in the Tour of Turkey, Patrick replying that this single victory would resonate more than Sam Bennett's two at the Tour de France the previous year, then, after a bit of back-and-forth, Mike finally conceding and saying he'd pay me €20,000.

Important to stress again: this was Patrick's version.

But on with the story. My wins in Turkey were a mira-cle in the media's eyes and in mine the end of a three-year nightmare. I was much less concerned with what it meant financially, but I was also on a modest €70,000 contract that I'd had to subsidise myself by bringing my own sponsor, Meatless Farm, on board at the start of the year. In addition to that, I'd sacrificed my longest-standing endorsement deal, with Nike, because Specialized had insisted that I wear their shoes. Hence Nike's bonus of €10,000 per win was also gone … thankfully to be replaced, or rather doubled, by the €20,000 that Specialized were going to pay. Or so I thought.

At the end of the Tour of Turkey, and after celebrating three further victories, I thought I'd already eclipsed my salary in bonuses. Apparently I was wrong; Patrick said he'd checked with Mike, whose message was that the €20,000 for the first stage win also 'covered' the other three. Quick maths: it'd be half of what I would have received from Nike. Of course, it wasn't really the value of the money that hurt, but that it seemed my Specialized bicycle wasn't the only one being taken for a ride.

We go forward to the 'present' day. To the 2021 Tour. I'd won four stages, taken my career total to 34, level with Eddy Merckx's all-time record. The French refer to the Champs-Elysées as 'the most beautiful avenue in the world'. It literally translates as 'the Elysian Fields', the eternal paradise in Greek mythology. It had also been my heaven on earth on four occasions in the Tour. With number 5 – and number 35 – I'd go beyond the gods, past the cycling Almighty Merckx, to a higher plane of immortality.

In the days leading up to Paris, I'd been vaguely aware of conversations happening between my then manager and Specialized. The team was trying to keep me insulated from whatever was going on, wanting me to stay focused on the racing, but word had filtered through that Specialized were preparing some kind of special-edition green bike to mark what they saw as my inevitable victory in the points competition. Mike Sinyard had even messaged me directly with some of the designs. They'd also sent a green bike for my son Casper, which was a nice gesture.

But there was more to it: Specialized wanted to produce and sell 35 of the bikes – one for each stage win, assuming I got the big one in Paris. And this was a problem for me, purely on principle: a few months earlier I'd offered Sinyard and Specialized the chance to subsidise my salary with the team in return for full use of my commercial image and they'd declined. Now they were apparently going to cash in on success that, apparently, a few months earlier they didn't believe I had in me.

The first of the special-edition bikes had arrived for me to use a few days before the final stage, but I'd politely declined to use it. That, I should stress, was not intended as a shot across anyone's bows. There was an element of superstition – a reluctance to tamper with anything that had been working so well – but also a pragmatic, professional determination not to take any unnecessary risk, certainly not on the altar of cosmetics or marketing. Some decisions are bigger than business. This was one of them.

Of course the punchline to all of this – and the punch in the stomach – was that I didn't win in Paris. Only that wasn't the end of it. Specialized still wanted to sell the limited-edition bike. And I wasn't backing down. Again, I was privy to only some of the conversations, vaguely aware of the background noise, as I set off on a sort of post-Tour victory lap of the exhibition races organised across northern Europe every year to celebrate the stars of the Tour de France. Several of them happened to take place in Belgium, which also gave Patrick the opportunity to invite me and Peta for a congratulatory dinner at one of his favourite restaurants and, indeed, by critical consensus, the finest in the land, the Hof van Cleve.

Even by Patrick's standards this was one classy joint. Until that summer, in fact, this had been the only restaurant in Belgium to ever earn a third Michelin star. The clientele was West Flandrian high society – all linen trousers, pastel shades and gold jewellery. The waiting list for a table is six months, although something tells me that this rule doesn't apply to Patrick Lefevere. In this part of the world, if cycling is king, Patrick is something like an emperor.

So a classic, opulent setting for a textbook Lefevere negotiation. Because that's what it was always going to turn into, after the champagne and the toast to my Tour. Again, quint-essential Lefevere – a break in the conversation, barely, then a little lean forward and, without any shift in tone or facial expression, a sudden and very deliberate change of subject. 'So, we need to talk about these green bikes ...'

What kind of cut did I think I was going to get from Specialized selling these bikes, Patrick wanted to know. I told him that wasn't the point. Money wasn't the point. My issue was that, way back the previous November, when I was without a team and Patrick told me he'd love to have me but couldn't afford to, I'd personally offered Specialized and Mike Sinyard a deal: they pay the team the €100,000 Patrick had asked for, of which I'd receive the €70,000 UCI minimum wage, do whatever they want with my name and brand, and I ride for Patrick's team. And they'd declined. So, needless to say, if they'd now decided that suddenly my image and name did have a value, I at least wanted that acknowledged. Which meant not just assuming that they could take what they hadn't paid for. I reminded him that I'd had several tough years before I rejoined his team, season after season with no wins and the prevailing media narrative one of a helpless has-been, yet even throughout all of that some of my long-term part-ners had continued to support me, pay me and, on top of that, go above and beyond to make sure I was well on a human level. Oakley, my sunglasses sponsor. Richard Mille, the watchmaker. Monster Energy. Nike. The last of which I'd had to lose as sponsor to join the team. How could I explain to them, I asked Patrick, that when I could finally offer another sponsor something to monetise, I was giving it away for free?

Hearing this, Patrick countered with, 'Well, Specialized are paying your bonuses from the Tour.' At which point a penny dropped: in his act of largesse on the eve of the Tour, the late-night summons downstairs to give me the good news that he was putting extra incentives on the table, could it have been that he'd neglected to mention that the money was coming from Specialized and not Bakala? Suddenly what I was understanding was that I had to do Specialized a favour because they'd done one for him – paying those bonuses that I'd thought until a couple of minutes earlier were coming from the team.

'They're not selling the bike,' I said flatly, my voice rising to the extent that the diners at the surrounding tables started to crane their necks, turn around or fiddle with their napkins in embarrassment. Peta, sitting next to me, prodded my knee under the table. The celebration dinner in the temple of Belgian gastronomy had suddenly become very awkward. I'd stated my position and nothing was going to change it. I forget what was on the dessert menu, but I can tell you the ambiance for the last part of the meal had turned distinctly, ahem, *semifreddo*.

Over the next few weeks there'd be no resolution. Brian Holm had obviously got the lowdown from Patrick. He called and told me that pride came before a fall, Patrick would make me regret it and so on. But I wasn't budging. As I said to Brian, my whole career, my whole identity, all of my business relationships had been built on a few core principles. Treating everyone who I'd put my trust in, and who'd shown me they reciprocated that in the same way, was one of those. Being correct. I didn't tolerate anything else from myself and I wouldn't tolerate it from other people.

All of which meant that we were at an impasse. Meanwhile, I carried on racing – at the Tour of Denmark, the Tour of Germany then the Tour of Britain. Before the latter, I was asked how long I thought I could stay competitive, at the same level, and I replied that, at age 36, I thought I could and would still improve. This led to another question about which team I'd be racing for in 2022. There I had to pause. 'I hope it'll be with Deceuninck, but I don't know …' The journalists no doubt thought I was being cagey. Mischievous. The fact was that, somehow, the deal I'd agreed with Patrick before the Tour had got lost in the post. In fact, since our fractious dinner date a few weeks earlier, Patrick had gone silent – except in the press where, as usual, there was never a blank page that he couldn't fill with a titillating soundbite. I'd known Patrick for a long time, learned over the years that interviews for him were a sort of parlour game, but one, ahem, outing in the middle of September, still gave me pause: 'I respect Mark Cavendish. We saved his skin. We gave him all the tools. He took the challenge and he did it. And now it begins. Now he thinks it is time to cash in again. Will he do the same again? That seems unlikely to me.'

It went on:

I can hardly give someone who wins four stages in the Tour and the green jersey, four stages in the Tour of Turkey and a stage in the Tour of Belgium the same wage as this year. Mark Cavendish has sky-high expectations in that regard and I'm very realistic. That's a difficult marriage.

The 2021 World Championships were happening in Belgium, and I'd been selected for the British team, albeit on a course that gave sprinters little chance. It ought to have been the perfect time and place to meet Patrick again and finally work things out, but the week came and went with no resolution. In professional cycling, the norm nowadays is for established, important riders to have the following year's contract agreed by the spring at the latest, even if a move to another team can't be formally announced until after 1 August. Yet here I now was with the autumn fast approaching, an agreement struck in June that seemed to have been forgotten, and a team manager now publicly suggesting there was more chance of me leaving than staying. In other interviews, he had also said that a sprinter he didn't take to the 2021 Tour, Fabio Jakobsen, was in fact the fastest in the world and Deceuninck–QuickStep's man for 2022.

I had three races left on my race programme – one in Germany, one in Belgium and then the British National Road Race Championships. Whether or not this had been his intention all along, I was starting to get nervous. So the day before the race in Germany, the Münsterland Tour, I decided to call him and ask, bluntly, why I still hadn't received the contract we'd agreed before the Tour de France.

Silence at the end of the phone. Then: 'What contract?'

I tried to keep my composure. 'Patrick, you remember … the contract we talked about before the Tour de France.'

He said he couldn't remember. That we'd have to discuss it in person. I should come and meet him in Belgium.

Was it all just some elaborate bluff? Was I being played? I couldn't know but felt something in me – a charge of energy – rising. The next day was one of those rare occasions in my career when I felt possessed, as though some almighty, supernatural force had taken over my brain and body, sequestered my central nervous system, installed a nuclear reactor in my legs. The playbook for nearly every one of my 150-odd race wins as a professional had been the same – an exercise in finding shelter, surfing wheels, letting the current of the peloton carry me until the last 200 metres. I'd ration every watt, ever so slowly turn the dial towards terminal velocity, then discharge anything and everything I had for 10, at a maximum 20 seconds. I was the ultimate one-trick pony, but it was one hell of a trick. On a handful of occasions, though, some magical alchemy of special motivation and fitness also gave me a very fleeting glimpse of what bike races could feel like for the real ballers, the champions, the legends. Guys like Pogačar or, in the past, Merckx and Hinault. On this day I felt like one of them, as though I could dictate and bend the bike race to my will. In the pouring rain, while all around me soaked rivals grimaced and whimpered, I became their teaser, their tormentor. Finally, four of us got clear in the final kilometres. Then, with my team-mate Josef Černý on lead-out duty, I won the sprint easily. In my post-race interviews, I dedicated the win to Heiko Salzwedel, a German who'd been one of my old coaches and supporters in British Cycling, and who had died the previous week. Heiko was also the reason that, for a few months in 2005 and 2006, I'd lived in Dortmund and got to know some of the roads we'd raced on that day.

• • •

We were now in October. When I looked back on the season I could scarcely believe how far I'd come, and, yet, in another way, I was right back where I'd been almost a year earlier: that's to say not even sure whether I'd ever race again. On

11 October 2020 those had been pretty much my exact, tearful words to a journalist after Gent-Wevelgem: 'This could be my last race now ...' That had been massive news but at the same time, to many, it sounded like the logical conclusion: a sad but maybe wise resolution after years of decline.

Now, after the 2021 I'd had, the idea that I would have to stop seemed ridiculous ... and yet, officially, I was teamless. At the risk of sounding melodramatic, or just sorry for myself, it felt a bit like the story of my career, or certainly like one of the recurring themes: no matter what I did, what I won or what I proved, I still seemed to find myself back *here* – that's to say fighting to stay alive, for my very right to *exist*.

As much as I'd tried and had dwelled on it over the years, I'd never been able to understand. When I was a kid, riding my first races, you could have said that my face just didn't fit – that I was lippy, chubby, didn't look the part, was a cycling ugly duckling. Maybe then it was obvious why some people didn't rate me or my chances of realising my dreams ... but somehow it had carried on. I'd won all that a sprinter could win and a few million – I certainly couldn't complain about that – but at every turn, it felt to me, I'd had to scrap, confound and convince an army of sceptics. The maxim 'let your legs do the talking' had never applied, because whatever resounding messages those legs sent always seemed to fall on deaf ears. The money itself wasn't the point, but what it *said* was often hard to ignore. I'd been in teams where guys had never come close to winning in major tours, sometimes not even come close to finishing on podiums, and yet I'd discover that they were earning twice, three times my wage. That is, their unfulfilled, in many cases never-to-be-fulfilled potential, was deemed to be worth several multiples of my *actual* historical output over a decade and more.

A year earlier, Patrick, in whose team I'd raced in pomp, had even asked me to send him a CV before he considered signing me, for fuck's sake. Now he'd spent months making me sweat again – just fucking with me, was how it felt. Finally, after Münsterland, he'd either had his fun or drawn things out long enough to give himself the upper hand in the next set of negotiations, and he summoned me to Belgium. There, again, I reminded him of the agreement we'd had before the Tour, for €500,000, and he said he had no recollection. I told him that, anyway, that was the price we'd discussed, and since then I'd won four stages at the Tour and the green jersey … so really I should be getting double, particularly as there were riders in the team who had won two, three races in their entire career and were on seven figures. Patrick shook his head apologetically: he only had €250,000 left in his budget. It was that or nothing, and, oh, by the way, even if I did take it, I wouldn't be the team sprinter at the Tour the following year.

I went away. Exasperated but also confident that I could call Patrick's bluff. A few days later I still hadn't flinched when

Tom Steels, the team's head directeur sportif, contacted me about arrangements for the pre-2022 team meeting that would take place in Belgium at the end of October. My response to this was that I wouldn't be coming, *obviously*, because I didn't have a contract. Ten minutes later and Patrick calls. I could sense him getting ever so slightly flustered. 'Just come and we'll sort it out. Honestly ...'

The whole saga had been frankly insulting, but I did end up travelling to Belgium and choosing a tack of transparency; I'd made my money over the previous decade and a half, I told Patrick, and now I was trying to make sure that riding for another year and the sacrifices it ensues would at least not be to the detriment of my family's future. Really, I was only focused on earning enough to pay my taxes, pay my kids' school fees and start saving for their first houses. That was it. 'Listen, Patrick,' I said, 'I know you say you don't remember it, but let's just settle on what we'd agreed before the Tour de France: €500,000. Almost half of that will go in tax, I'm worth much more, and you're getting a hell of a deal, but I'd rather just stop this silly back and forth now and get on with figuring out how we're going to win next year.'

Somehow Patrick always found a way to make sure he felt like the winner, and here he'd done it again. I'd blinked first and, ultimately, should have held out for €750,000. But I was 'happy' in the sense that I was making an investment in however much 'future' I still had left as a pro bike rider: this was a team in which I could win races, as the previous few months had shown, and it was that – success – that would give me choices and freedom further down the line.

And so ended the 2021 season – the most extraordinary of my career by most people's estimates, but maybe not everyone's. Not Patrick Lefevere's apparently.

CHAPTER 2

There were many ways in which 2021 had felt like a rebirth, a new start in my career, but as the season ended I only had to look around to remind myself that the passing years knew neither pause nor mercy. Many of the riders who had begun their careers in the mid-noughties, like me, had already retired, and more were following as 2021 came to a close. I could remember meeting the German Tony Martin and the American Tejay van Garderen for the first time at team training camps, me already a young but established star, them freshly arrived in the pro ranks, and yet in 2022 they'd both begin new lives as former racing cyclists. Another ex-team-mate and, in fact, adversary turned friend, André Greipel, had said his farewells at the Münsterland Tour that I'd won in October. The best two Irish riders of a generation, Dan Martin and Nicholas Roche, both more or less my age, had also just bowed out.

Squint hard enough, of course, and you could see every autumn as the end of an era, but there was no doubt that seeing contemporaries depart felt a bit like watching the closing credits of a movie we'd starred in together. It could make you nostalgic but also reflect on the mark you'd be leaving, and not just what you'd managed to extract either in terms of money or plaudits or prestige.

I can't pretend that I spent long days or even hours pondering my own legacy in the wake of the 2021 Tour, but my lasting contribution to the sport was something that I'd always tried to take seriously. Few sports are as attached to their own history and heritage as cycling, and I'd always felt that to have a career as a pro rider was also to enter into a kind of silent and sacred covenant whereby you committed to preserving some of the sport's hallowed traditions. These could be small, seemingly insignificant things, like attending the annual Tour de France route presentation. Or observing certain non-written rules like not attacking in a feed-zone or when the leader of a stage race had stopped for a 'nature break'. They could seem like trivial nods to antiquated protocols, but knitted together, they made up the DNA, the very soul of the sport. They were what, as a kid discovering this weird and exotic world for the first time, intrigued and captivated you – the magic and romance. Now, as a dad, and particularly with a kid, Casper, already under the sport's spell, I saw it as an honour and duty to help preserve some of this mystique.

All of which helps to explain why, come the second week of November, I was hyperventilating in a smoky Belgian velodrome rather than sunning myself on a beach in Mallorca. If that genetic code that I've just described is also made up of sacred places, events and what I suppose you'd call institutions, the Gent Six-Day represents all three of those things. And, if we're going to agree that people are also part of the same heritage, the Keisses are one of those families that deserve historic monument status.

Iljo had been my team-mate during both of my spells at QuickStep. His dad, Ronie, used to be the track manager at the Kuipke velodrome, which has hosted the Gent Six since 1927. Ronie practically brought Iljo up on the boards of the Kuipke, eventually seeing him make the grade as a professional and, eventually, become a Gent Six legend. In fact, *the* Gent Six legend – 'the King of Gent' or 'Kuipke Keizer' as the media would christen him. In few places could one take a bigger gulp of cycling essence than in the Kuipke when Iljo was racing the Gent Six – or, when the evening's racing was over, in the bar that Ronie now ran just across the street from the velodrome, De Karper.

I'd raced my first Gent Six even before turning pro and had been immediately intoxicated. The fans that choked the track centre, the intermingling aromas of booze, fags and massage oil, the competing sounds of the DJ's thudding Eurobeats, the crowd's oohs and aahs and the air whistling through my ear canal – the whole sensory onslaught was like nothing else. For this reason, even while focusing on the road and usually finishing my season in October, I'd often made the time and drawn on whatever energy was left to race in Gent in November. It was a good excuse to stay in shape at a time of the year when, yes, the sun lounger might otherwise beckon. Also, quite simply, as I've just explained, it was utterly exhilarating – probably the closest you could get in cycling to feeling like a rock star in a packed concert hall.

But it was also about something else for me now. Giving back. Honouring those traditions. Worshipping at one of the altars of the sport. There was no better way to do any of this than race in partnership with the 'King of Gent', and so when, a few months earlier, Iljo had first talked to me about pairing up in November, I hadn't hesitated. It was like Frank Sinatra asking you to sing a duet at Madison Square Garden.

There was just one issue. Iljo expected – and was expected – to win, whereas I, to put it bluntly, didn't and was not. The format of six-day racing isn't easy to explain, but, for the purposes of brevity, let's just say that pairs race in a pick 'n' mix of track disciplines, scoring points that count towards a final classification at the end of the six nights. I'd won the overall title once, racing with Sir Bradley Wiggins in 2016. Iljo had been in the winning pair seven times.

Now, when we got together on the day before the racing started, he looked me up and down with a smile that I'd describe as … quizzical. So much so that I felt the immediate need to reassure him: I wasn't kidding myself – I didn't think we'd be winning, but I wouldn't embarrass him either. 'We won't be getting lapped, Iljo. We'll still be one of the best four or five pairs …'

He looked reassured. Kind of.

But was I in for a shock. And Iljo was in for an unpleasant surprise. Or maybe confirmation of what he'd feared. On the first night I took an absolute pounding. Almost every lap was torture, every breath a blowtorch under my ribcage … At one point, after several pretty comprehensive beatings, Iljo decided, for some reason that escaped me, that we could get ourselves back into contention by gaining laps in one of the Madisons. This is the most iconic and, for the layman, baffling six-day discipline. One that I'd been World Champion in three times during my career. A sort of hybrid of relay racing and ballroom dancing where partners can arm-sling each other into or out of the race depending on their respective levels of fatigue and also strategy. Here, now, without asking me, and maybe just swept along by the adrenaline, Iljo was suddenly jettisoning our conservative, realistic plan and wanting to go gangbusters. Put simply, he kept attacking and slinging me in to try and lap the bunch when I was circling the top of the track, trying to talk my lungs down from the ceiling.

'Cav, let's goooo …'

'NOO, Iljo, for fuck's sake! NOOO. Stop fucking throwing me in …!'

'Cavvv! Come ON!'

'Stop fucking shouting at me, Iljo! I can't go any harder …'

And so on and so on. Lap after lap. In fact, night after night. To the point that, at the end of one of the sessions, I stormed out. Told Iljo he could stick it; that I was done. Bagged up all my kit in the cabins in the track centre where we can get changed and rest between races and marched off towards the exit. It took the, ahem, intervention and a pep talk from one of our soigneurs to bring me back. Iljo and I also immediately made up. He was just very ... passionate about Gent. And I'd have been the biggest hypocrite in East Flanders if I couldn't empathise with a bike rider wanting to win so badly that he momentarily lost his rag in the heat of battle.

After five nights it was pretty clear that Iljo wasn't going to get his eighth crown, but we'd saved face. We were in fourth place overall, so it hadn't been a disaster. At least that was until the night's final session. We were riding the last Madison, the last few minutes of racing, when, a few metres and four riders in front of me, I saw the Belgian Kenny DeKetele suddenly skid, and the rider behind him swing wildly to the right and up the track to get out of the way. Rule number one of track racing – and the reflex you're taught before pretty much anything else – is to steer up the boards and not down when you sense danger. Which is exactly what I'd done here, but not quickly or far enough to avoid the dominoes already falling in front of me, and specifically the Dane Lasse Norman Hansen. Within a second or two, after the ominous crack of metal on metal and then wood, I was combat-rolling back down the slope while my bike somersaulted through the air and over my head.

Over the years, unfortunately, as the crashes multiply, you also develop an instinct for their severity – and I could tell instantly this was a bad one. For six nights, my body and senses had felt electrified. Now I lay immobile and numb, all the noise draining away. In one leg I'd lost all feeling. Trying to breathe was like being stabbed from the inside out. Faces, some familiar and some not, then started to gather over me. An ambulance was apparently going to take me away. Suddenly, I remembered that Peta and the kids were in the velodrome; I had to get up, somehow reassure them, so I allowed myself to be pulled to my feet. I waved in their direction, and at the crowd applauding me. I was then helped towards our cabin in the track centre, where, behind a curtain so that no one could see, the paramedics put an oxygen mask over my nose and mouth. I could tell already I'd broken one, probably several ribs. My bigger concern at this point was my right leg. There, I ... couldn't feel anything.

It turned out that the crash had been caused by some liquid on the track – a leak from one of the bottles a rider had taken from a soigneur. I might have escaped unhurt but I'd landed on the end of one of the other fallen riders' carbon handlebars. It also turned out that my leg was fine – just 'dead' in the sense of badly bruised. That'd heal in no time. Of bigger concern to the doctors were my lungs, which hadn't been punctured by the broken ribs but ripped from the chest wall. My long-term health wasn't in jeopardy, but I had been rushed to intensive care – and put on some pretty intensive painkilling medication. Suffice it to say that, that night, I had a very good, if somewhat aided sleep. To be honest it felt more like flying.

I'd be kept in hospital for a couple of days. The next challenge, before the rehab, was a logistical one – getting back to the UK. I'd come to Belgium in my car but now couldn't drive, so Peta had taken the family home, then got on a flight to Belgium so that she could be my chauffeur. The team were brilliant, picking her up at the airport, making everything as easy as possible. Soon enough we were on the Eurotunnel and, a couple of hours after that, back in our house in Essex.

The rest of that evening was unremarkable. It would have been forgettable but unfortunately it was not to be forgotten, given the postscript. In the early hours, a gang of armed robbers broke into our home while we were asleep. The terms 'nightmare' and 'trauma' are so commonly used that they can often lose their meaning, but here both accurately describe not only a few harrowing minutes but the hours, days, months and even years of their aftermath. We, as a family, are still processing the ordeal as I write today.

I had to continue travelling to races and training camps, leaving my family alone in the house. If there was ever anything in 2021 that would have made me stop everything, get out – clearly much more than equalling or beating any record – it was the fear of that November night repeating itself.

CHAPTER 3

The final weeks of 2021 had brought me face to face with a different sort of fear from the one I was used to encountering. It's often been said that professional cycling is the least recognised of all 'extreme sports' – as fast at times as motorsport or downhill skiing, and with protagonists clad not in leathers or Gore-Tex but gossamer-thin Lycra designed for one thing: to go faster.

Then, within road cycling lies the sub-discipline of sprinting, where the risks are even higher. My QuickStep team-mate Fabio Jakobsen knew all about this. A tall, powerfully built Dutchman, he'd turned pro with the team in 2018 and immediately been set on the fast-track towards superstardom, the latest sprinting prodigy off Patrick Lefevere's now multi-decade production line. In 2019, Fabio rode his first Grand Tour, the Vuelta a España, and immediately won two stages. It seemed only a matter of time before Patrick sent Fabio to the Tour de France, but then his momentum was abruptly, shockingly halted at the Tour of Poland in 2020. As Fabio and another Dutchman, Dylan Groenewegen of the Jumbo–Visma team, sprinted for the line on stage two, wheel-to-wheel, Groenewegen moved to the right, unintentionally causing Fabio to crash into the advertising hoardings just a few metres before the finish line. The resulting impact was horrific, sending barrier fences, Fabio and his bike cartwheeling. Fabio came to rest just underneath the finish-line arch, having struck it with his face. I was also racing that day, not quite managing to sprint on the other side of the road from where the collision happened. The impact was horrifying, the noise like a bomb going off.

That night, we at the race and the whole cycling world held our breath, having heard that Fabio was fighting for his life. The next day, thankfully, he regained consciousness. He'd fractured his skull, broken his nose, lost ten teeth and part of his jaw – but the signs were that, providing he could overcome the psychological trauma, he'd one day be able to resume his career.

Thankfully that proved to be the case. My destiny and Fabio's also seemed to be somehow linked in the sense that, for both of us, the 2021 Tour of Turkey represented a miraculous comeback, the end of a long ordeal. It was his first race after Poland and the crash the previous year and also my rebirth as a bike rider. I hadn't won anything in three years, had been written off, dismissed as a has-been – but that week, with a bit of help from Fabio in the lead-out, I was in peak form. Fast-forward three months, our team's first-choice sprinter, Sam Bennett, was having knee trouble, and Patrick decided a few days before the Tour to replace Sam with me. The four stage wins and my green jersey – you know the rest. That Tour came too early for Fabio but he did go to the last Grand Tour of the 2021 season, the Vuelta a España. There, he was the dominant sprinter, winning three stages. Some even suggested that his performances in Spain proved not only that he was back to his best and had overcome the trauma but that he may also be the fastest sprinter in the world.

I'd never seen Fabio as a 'rival' but you didn't have to be Einstein to work out what the media narrative around our team was going to be as we went into 2022. Whether it had been a negotiating tactic or not, Patrick had also fanned the flames with his comments to the press at the end of 2021. Fabio was the coming man, had been the general gist. The team would take one sprinter to the Tour de France ... and at the moment that slot was Fabio's to lose. It made sense, Patrick pointed out, given that Fabio was 25 and had two more years on his contract. He'd also proven himself by winning three stages of the Vuelta at the end of 2021. Everyone loves a comeback story, and I'd delivered a humdinger for the team at the 2021 Tour. But this one had even more emotional charge, even more pathos. I'd only risen from the dead in cycling terms; Fabio had nearly lost his actual life. Him winning at the Tour would be a real redemption arc.

To give Patrick his due, he'd also spelled it out, face-to-face. when we finally signed my contract extension at the end of 2021. As things stood, Fabio was Plan A as far as the Tour de France was concerned. Patrick didn't put it in these terms, but it would basically be up to me to change his mind. I was essentially in the same position as a year earlier, when Sam Bennett had been the reigning green jersey champion. Partly through Sam's bad luck, partly through the force of my will, I'd managed to squeeze myself through the door and edge him out. Now I'd have to do the same thing for the second season in a row.

Cold logic suggested I could and should have felt indignant. Dropping a sprinter who a few months earlier had won four stages of the Tour would be akin to benching a striker whose hat-trick and man-of-the-match performance have just secured you the Champions League. Patrick knew this, I knew it. So why was I 'accepting' it, or at least not kicking up a fuss? Well, mainly because the recent precedent of 2021 exemplified that, as that famous cycling pundit Robert Burns once said, the best laid plans of mice and men often go awry. Crashes, illness, bad form – every year, in every team, these imponderables could make a mockery of what had been sketched out at training camps in the winter. Picking a Tour team in January was like packing a case for a holiday six months away, without knowing whether you were going skiing or surfing.

I also tried to be philosophical for other reasons. Maybe, after all these years, I'd simply become desensitised to adversity. The last few, in particular, had felt like a relentless game of whack-a-mole with all the setbacks and people writing me off. I'd either become used to or numb to it. Once I would have responded with unvarnished and outspoken defiance. Now I was more inclined to smile and silently nod, knowing that I'd have the last laugh. It wasn't necessarily that I'd mellowed or 'gained perspective' – although that's a line journalists love to peddle about older athletes. I simply couldn't be bothered to engage; it was a waste of energy that could be better deployed once again proving those doubters wrong.

I also had to be professional. No one likes a diva or a disruptor. I'd always prided myself on being a team player, the basic principle being that a rising tide lifts all boats. This was also the ethos of the team. Moreover, I admired Fabio for what he'd achieved and overcome. These were genuine feelings – but equally, and you could even say cynically, I was well aware that, seen from the outside, it would have been a very bad look for me to be unsupportive of Fabio or lobby hard for my own inclusion in the Tour team at his expense.

And so we gathered, like every year, for the team's preseason training camp in Calpe on Spain's Costa Blanca. A year earlier this was where my rebirth had started – and now I got the sense that people wanted to bury me. One day on the January camp was always designated the 'media day', with the whole team and management basically available for journalists who had flown in from all over Europe or the world to ask questions. These would be my first interviews with the cycling press for a few months – and I didn't need much of a briefing to realise that the main item on the agenda would be the Tour de France, and the sprinters' 'power struggle' between me and Fabio.

What the journalists didn't know was that the mind games had already started. At least on Fabio's side, that is. That was my distinct impression from that camp. At this point the injuries from my crash in Gent were still healing and I'd only just got back into training. Call it paranoia, but I could swear on some of the group rides, when the road went uphill, Fabio was trying to ratchet up the pace. Taller and heavier than me, he was no ski-lift in the mountains, either, but it looked to me suspiciously as though he was trying hard to make me suffer. In one respect he was also succeeding, but in another the only person he was benefitting was me: when he accelerated, on every little rise I was puffing like a dragon with hiccups, but going that deep was also the perfect tonic for my form and fitness.

One night, after dinner, a few of the staff and a couple of the riders decanted into the hotel bar, and I found myself having a beer with one of our directeurs sportif, Tom Steels, himself a former Tour de France sprinter. Tom told me he'd already given Fabio a pep-talk about the coming season and the Tour in particular. Specifically, in relation to me, he'd warned Fabio, 'Don't just assume that you'll be our sprinter at the Tour, just because that's what Patrick's said and what's planned. Cav is going to push you to the limit ...'

Maybe Tom had made Fabio anxious. Equally, it may have looked to others as though I was the insecure one. That year the team had done a deal with a production company to make a fly-on-the wall documentary charting the team's season for Amazon Prime. As soon as I heard this, I knew how my 'rivalry' with Fabio might be spun, and I was on my guard. One day at camp the crew announced that they intended to stage and film a full-on drag race between us. I flat out refused. I'd been training for two weeks, so would obviously get beaten. It was galling enough to have been 'sidelined' after becoming the most successful sprinter in Tour history without my efforts to get fit being made into fodder for the peanut gallery. Maybe I wasn't giving the filmmakers enough credit. Maybe their motives were pure and they were just, well, doing what documentary makers are supposed to do: document. But I didn't want to take the risk.

Then, finally, media day arrived. Sometimes before these we'd get a briefing from the press officer, but this time, first, I decided to have a quiet word with Fabio in his room. My main bit of advice was the following: resist all bait to get you to talk about the Tour. 'Give them one quote about that and it'll be the narrative of your whole season. Every race, every interview, they'll ask you about me if you give them any encouragement now. So shut it down. Trust me, I've had this for years. I know how it works …'

The riders had been split into three groups, three time slots, with Fabio in the second and me in third. He'd looked as though he'd taken what I'd said onboard, but then I found out otherwise: as I waited outside the conference room that'd been set up for the interviews, our team press officer came outside and asked how I was going to respond when they asked me about the Tour … because Fabio had just confirmed that he was going. Hearing this, I snapped and removed the mic the documentary crew had asked me to wear from my collar. The last audio it picked up may have been a flurry of expletives.

The reporters' questions about the Tour now got a mumbled, opaque response. When the Tour was tentatively broached, they could tell from my body language that it would be wise to change the subject. By comparison, as I latter discovered when I read the translated quotes, Fabio had been positively loquacious with the Dutch-speaking press.

'He [Cav] knows that the Tour is my goal and that he will ride the Giro.'

'He is ready as a reserve for the Tour …'

'I think he's happy with being a reserve …'

I was stunned.

Fabio had made his own bed and also mine. Just as I'd predicted, and just as I'd told him, in every interview from that moment until the Tour, we were both doomed: we'd always be asked about one another and whatever we said would get twisted or spun into some kind of slight against the other, or dismissed as 'PR fluff' or an outright lie.

The only available path for me at that point was at least clear: I would let my legs do the talking. Which was easier said than done, because I felt that in some ways the team had set me up to fail. My race programme per se wasn't too much of an issue: being sent to the Giro d'Italia in May would jeopardise a lot of riders' chances of being fit for the Tour, but I'd proved in the past that I could ride and excel in both. The issue was more that I'd be given Fabio's 'leftovers', not so much in terms of schedule but other 'resources'.

I don't think anyone, at this point in my career, could be under any misapprehension about how important my teams had been to my success. The previous year's Tour had exemplified that. I'd say it and reiterate it in interviews, ad nauseam, to the extent where some people thought that it was maybe a kind of virtue signalling. But one scene from that year's Tour had been witnessed by everyone – the whole world watching on TV – and, in a couple of seconds, a few words, encapsulated exactly how I felt: Tim Declercq slowing to congratulate me after my second stage win of the

2021 Tour in Châteauroux, blurting, 'You're in the form of your life' – and my instinctive response: 'No, I'm in the team of my life.'

So, yes, a sprinter needs his team, relies on his team – a team whose roles are no less specialised than his own. And, well, at those first races of the 2022 season, let's just say that I was 'allocated' a lot of good riders, great lads but hardly anyone with real expertise and experience in the fine art of leading out sprints. My trusted lead-out man from the previous year, Michael Mørkøv, had been 'reassigned' to Fabio. Only at two races before the Giro did Mørky and I line up at a race together, in the UAE Tour and Milano–Torino. And in both of them I managed to win.

In the circumstances, despite having to play catch-up in my preparation, it was turning into a good start to the season. In training, my numbers were even better than the previous year. Equally, though, Fabio had started the season like a house on fire, winning twice at the Volta a la Comunitat Valenciana, twice at the Volta ao Algarve, again at Kuurne–Brussels–Kuurne and at Paris–Nice. Outside of the cycling bubble, these weren't necessarily important races or even a good gauge of anything that was likely to happen at the Tour, where everyone would be fitter and faster, the stakes would be higher, and a lot of riders would buckle under the pressure. And, yet, for the same members of the media who had cattle-prodded Fabio into discussing my holiday plans for July, our head-to-head win tally throughout the spring was an endless source of titillation.

．．．

If there had been a clear before and after in Fabio Jakobsen's career – everything pivoting in that split second when he felt Dylan Groenewegen's right shoulder on his arm at the Tour of Poland – it was remarkable or at least curious that I felt exactly the same about a similar incident and its aftermath for my life.

The fork in Fabio's road had come at the Tour of Poland, mine at the Tour de France. The year was 2017, and I was 32 years old. At the previous year's Tour, my first with Dimension Data, I'd won four stage stages, taking my career total to 30. Twelve months on, 200 metres from the finish line of stage four in Vittel, I already *knew* that was about to rise to 31. I kicked and my legs practically snarled, devouring the tarmac under my tyres. I was poised on Arnaud Démare's wheel, ready to go straight past him on the inside as he veered to the centre of the road, when Peter Sagan came from the left and made contact. There was his elbow, then the barriers, followed by both me and my bike gambolling across the road and coming to rest in a pile. Démare won the stage, Sagan got disqualified, and I broke my shoulder and was out of the race. My win counter at the Tour would also remain stuck on 30 for the next four years.

For most athletes, the lack of success itself would have been dramatic. In my case, it was mainly a symptom but also a contributor to a much more serious malaise, one that enveloped my whole life and not just my identity and legacy as a professional cyclist.

The Sagan crash may have been a turning point, but there had also been a prelude, a slow drip of subtle warning signs over the previous few months. With hindsight, I'd come to see a stage of the Abu Dhabi Tour in the February as the first of them. That race traditionally featured one summit finish to Jebel Hafeet, and every year I'd use it as my own private test of my condition. In 2017 I was light, fit, well-trained ... and yet something on the climb that day just felt 'off'. I could push up to a certain point but then my heart, lungs and muscles seemed to hit a roadblock. Something seemed odd, but I could dismiss it as just a strange, bad day ... until I went to Tirreno–Adriatico a couple of weeks later and it happened again. Absurd as it sounds in retrospect, at first I was convinced it must be a problem with my bike, that maybe my brake pads were rubbing on my rims. At Milan–Sanremo I just couldn't accelerate and finished the race minutes behind the lead group, completely mystified as to what was wrong. My bike had been checked, double-checked, triple-checked. If there really was an issue, it must be me ... and so I got a blood test. A day or two later I was sitting at the kitchen table in my house in Tuscany when my phone bleeped. A text message from the team doctor. 'Cav, you've got Epstein–Barr.'

I'd heard of it, but it was never really anything I'd been massively aware of. But for a few weeks, unknowingly, I'd been familiarising myself with the symptoms. Now I learned that the only remedy was rest. Several weeks off the bike. As for the causes, well, I'd never get firm answers, but I couldn't say I hadn't been warned when, the previous autumn, I'd talked my directeur sportif, Rolf Aldag, through my plans for the winter. No break after the previous season, Six Days of Gent, the London Six Days … then two training camps with the team, *then* starting my season at the Dubai Tour in January. I remember Rolf puffing out his cheeks, as if to say, 'Wow, that's a lot. Are you sure?' I'll never know whether, in fact, I'd weakened my immune defences by overstraining myself, but it certainly couldn't be ruled out.

It would be a race against time to get ready for the Tour – a race to *rest enough* – but, finally, in mid-June, I was given the green light to race again at the Tour of Slovenia. I passed that test, then stalled at the British National Championships, where I started brilliantly but then had my race wrecked by diarrhoea.

The 2017 Tour was starting in Düsseldorf. I had no results, no confidence, no certainties – just a blood test saying that, finally, I was healthy again and good to go. Then on stage two, I kicked behind Marcel Kittel, ultimately couldn't come around him but knew, immediately, that I was going to be OK. In fact, more than that, I knew that it was only a matter of days before I won.

Then, two days later, came Vittel, Sagan's right arm and everything changed. Literally *everything* changed.

The next two years, even three years are hard to explain. They're also hard to revisit as the very act of talking about them, thinking about them, writing about them, sucks me back towards that vortex into which my life disappeared. *Actually* disappeared, because for much of that period I didn't exist. Life around me didn't stop, and in fact at times got faster, more frenetic, creating a spiral of chaos in which I just sat, motionless, *emotion*-less, numb, *dead*, as the months and eventually years slid by. Once, I hadn't believed in depression or mental health problems. When I heard someone complain about them, I might feign sympathy, but internally I was thinking, *Yeah, right, toughen up* ... Now, seemingly without warning, I came face to face with an enemy I couldn't name, couldn't explain and couldn't defeat with any of the tools that had previously made me worthwhile, let alone successful or admired.

Even the timeline is difficult to piece together. I can only speculate, but my guess is that my shoulder injury in the Tour left my body in a depleted state again. Then, eventually, the virus, the Esptein–Barr, which never leaves your body but lies dormant, flared up again. And that exacerbated the depression – or maybe it was the depression that caused the Epstein–Barr. I'm guessing, and no one could ever give me definitive answers, as I've found is pretty much always the case with mental health. To someone as logic-orientated as me, that made it doubly confusing, and doubly infuriating. Not to mention embarrassing. How could I, the man who was forever preaching that the only response to any problem was to immediately look for a solution, be so utterly bereft? Why couldn't I just try a bit harder?

Of course, in reality, I did little else but search for answers. My shoulder eventually healed and I came back to racing in the autumn of 2017, only to feel exactly as I had earlier in the year: somehow muffled or blocked. The team doctors said that they'd checked everything and I was fine. I'd been a pro for ten years and knew how I *should* feel with this amount of training, and this wasn't it. I worked harder – and got worse, not better. Sometimes I could hear or sense others questioning whether, at 32, I'd simply gone off the 'age cliff', as every rider did at some point in their thirties. I'd entertain the idea for a split second … then check myself. That *couldn't be* the explanation. I could lose some speed, a bit of agility, a few watts, but not this. Not overnight. There must be something else.

The 2018 season gave me the chance to reboot. It also started with a win at the Dubai Tour in February … but something still wasn't right. I got worse in my next race, the

Tour of Oman, then crashed on stage one and abandoned the Abu Dhabi Tour with a concussion. A week after that, a mechanical failure would send me crashing onto my face at Tirreno–Adriatico, and although I managed to remount and dizzily cross the finish line, I would suffer a time cut in the team time trial. Another DNF – 'Did Not Finish' – followed at Milan–Sanremo after I crashed at high speed into a central reservation bollard, somersaulting across the road. And another one after that at the Tour de Yorkshire.

Desperate times call for desperate measures and, in cycling, when performances go south, that usually means you need to do one of two things (or both): train harder and/or lose weight. I was already doing the former so now I doubled down on the latter. Holed up in my house in Tuscany, I 'went monk', cutting out all indulgences. I lost one kilogram, then two and three … and it became addictive. I may not have been back to full power on the bike but at least, for the first time in a year, I could see some progress just by virtue of the fact that my watts-to-weight ratio was improving. In my mind, every kilo lost was a baby-step closer to success, and so I started weighing myself every day, then twice a day, three times a day and sometimes even four. Obsessively pinching the skin on my lower abdomen. I'd started by reducing portion sizes, then progressed to replacing meals: instead of a bowl of cereal in the morning, I'd have a bar. Then eventually I'd replace the replacement – forego the cereal bar and just have a coffee.

The team medical staff and coaches would look at my training files and say I still wasn't where I needed to be, and had to train more; I knew that was nonsense – but I could up the ante by bringing my weight down *even* further.

I imagine people reading this will fall into two categories: those from outside the professional cycling bubble who'll be shocked, maybe appalled, and those from *inside* who'll shrug and say, 'Well, yeah, of course.' Telling the second group that disordered eating is endemic in pro cycling would be like sending a group memo to the world penguin population, informing them that ice is cold. Ever since I'd arrived in the pro peloton, I'd estimate that well in excess of 50 per cent of conversations I'd had with other riders had started in exactly the same way: with a question – either 'How are you?' or 'How's it going?' – and then some sort of observation about how 'skinny' or not the other person was looking. Like clockwork. Almost without fail. Even with staff it was the same. 'You OK? Where did I last see you? Sanremo? Flanders? Looking skinny anyway …' And this would be *me* to the mechanic, not the other way around.

Of course, these were meant as compliments. The ultimate compliment in fact. Skinny was *always* better. Except when, in fact, you were completely malnourished, and also driving yourself insane by obsessively grasping for an illusion of control. Thinking that by suppressing or overriding your appetite you could restore some order to your life. In other words, exactly where I was in the summer of 2018, with two then undiagnosed illnesses on top, to compound matters – Epstein–Barr virus and, I'd be told later, clinical depression.

The crazy thing is that I felt bullish before the Tour, almost entirely because of what the scales were saying: 66 kilograms, 10 kilograms lighter than what I'd weighed in 2016, 6 kilos lighter than what was usually my ideal weight, and 3 or 4 lighter than I'd been in my most productive years with HTC and Team Sky. I remember a conversation with Rod Ellingworth, who was then still with Sky, in a car park before the Grand Départ in the Vendée. 'All right, mate, looking skinny …' Truth be told, though, Rod was alarmed by how thin I'd got, so much so that he later told Peta that we – I – had a problem.

At the time, while still knowing deep down that something was amiss, I clung to the hope of a miracle turnaround, and to various other delusions. Maybe I *would* forsake some power in the early sprints but I'd fly over the mountains and therefore be fresher than the other sprinters later in the Tour. Maybe something would just click, inspire me. Becoming a dad for the third time, for example, which I did when Casper was born at the end of May … But that's not exactly how things turned out. After a wretched first week – with no results and my relationship with the team manager, Doug Ryder, degenerating to a new, lowest ebb – we arrived at the first stage in the Alps. My old mate Geraint Thomas won it ... while my worst Tour de France nightmare unfolded: finishing outside the time limit, grovelling across the line over an hour after Geraint, more than half an hour too late to stay in the race. It was zero consolation that my biggest rival of the previous few seasons, Marcel Kittel, had suffered the same fate. Rod tried to offer some comfort, some support, by waiting by the finish line to encourage me up the final slope. I was grateful ... but sentiment couldn't change the bottom line: I was out of the Tour.

The next few months represent another black hole in my memory, in my life, my soul. I was alive but not present, not *living*. My diagnoses brought some relief in that they provided clarity, a reason to forgive myself. But that wasn't enough to get me better. Peta suffered, the family suffered ... but at times I also felt alone, unsupported. I was advised that anti-depressants, Prozac, could be, if not *the* answer, then at least something that would stop me spiralling. Perhaps provide a solid platform from which to rebuild. But I didn't take them, for personal reasons – Peta and I knew people with mental health problems who'd had negative experiences with medication. I've since realised that anti-depressants are widely taken by pro bike riders, some of whom have even talked to me about their beneficial effects, not only in life but also in racing. One rider said that when he was taking Prozac, his head stopped checking out before his legs on hard climbs. The negative voice, that urge to let go, was gone. He saw possibilities everywhere, not barriers. Hearing this later it made me wonder how different things might have been if I'd gone with the advice. Because, objectively, according to various tests and assessments in that period, I did *need* to be on the medication. But I kept resisting. Ultimately I never wanted to become reliant on a pill for my mental health and happiness. Whether or not that was the right way of looking at it.

The Epstein–Barr was 'easier' to manage in that, with enough rest, my body finally started to inch back towards full health. At first the blood tests were weekly, then fortnightly, then monthly. I was still barely on speaking terms with the Dimension Data team manager, Doug Ryder, who'd offered me an extension in early 2018 then, after the relationship breakdown at the Tour, backtracked and completely changed the terms when it was too late to search for another team. The 2019 season was supposed to be a 'fresh start' … although it soon started to look a lot like the season before, my *annus horribilis*. I pulled to the roadside midway through stage two of Paris–Nice in March, got into a team car and honestly didn't know when or even if I'd race again. I shook team-mates' and staff members' hands that night as though it was the last time we'd see each other. Apparently even Rolf Aldag, my directeur sportif at the time and the biggest supporter and mentor throughout my career, told people that I might be calling it a day.

Over the previous few months I'd gradually isolated myself, often with the excuse of training, in Mallorca or Italy. Now I retreated to the Isle of Man. The team decided to give me one last chance, or themselves one last shot at saving their investment. Since the start of the season they'd been working with an Australian 'high-performance cognitive specialist' called David Spindler. Now he was dispatched to the island to talk with me, reason with me, somehow work his magic. Years earlier, periodically, I'd spoken to Dr Steve Peters, the psychologist credited with some of British Cycling's success, but I'd never been fully convinced that I was a good candidate for this sort of help or treatment. Was a sports psychologist *really* trying to understand me, or were they judging me? Fundamentally, I didn't like giving away control, as my attitude to medication also demonstrated. Hence, for the first day or so, with Spindler, I was positively frosty. That eventually thawed to mild diffidence until, finally, after a couple of days, there was a breakthrough of sorts when I allowed myself to show some vulnerability. I showed him where I'd ridden my first races in 1995, aged nine – on the track at the Isle of Man National Sports Centre. We talked about what cycling had meant for me. Freedom. Structure in my life. Identity. Self-esteem and joy. Community. We also talked about what I'd lost over the previous few months – mainly that joy but also the identity and self-esteem. It would be wrong to call it a eureka moment, but maybe a flame that felt all but extinguished started to flicker. I felt that Spindler at least sympathised; he wasn't merely there with the ulterior motive of getting the team and sponsors more bang for their buck. He encouraged me to ride for riding's sake, for the love of it. No structure, no targets, at least initially – just the goal of reconnecting with the feelings and places that I associated with a simpler, happier time.

Within a few weeks I was back racing, back thinking about the Tour. In the spring I was due to ride the Tour of Norway but had a better idea: some of the Team INEOS riders, including my mate Luke Rowe, were going to train at altitude, at Isola 2000, in the mountains above Nice. Riding with Luke was nourishment for the soul. You'd do a couple of hours then he'd announce we were stopping for lunch, which with him meant diving into an Intermarché, buying a baguette and some ham, then eating them sitting on a curb in the car park. Old school. Like when we were 15 years old. I'd also never properly tried altitude training, which was quickly becoming a rite of passage not only for GC riders but more or less everyone riding Grand Tours. I made the case to Rolf Aldag – and he gave the green light.

Caleb Ewan, the Australian sprinter, had had a similar plan, but that changed at the last minute; the apartment he'd rented at Isola 2000 was now free, so he said I could take it. The whole set-up was perfect – long days riding over huge Alpine passes with Luke and another INEOS rider, Owain

Doull, and evenings spent playing cards, telling stories, having a laugh. Again – food for the soul. Except it lasted only a few days, until a coach there to help the INEOS lads, an Aussie named Leigh Bryan but better known to everyone as 'Rok', pulled me aside one day and said we needed to talk. We had a problem, he said. The INEOS management didn't want me training with their riders. Nothing personal, Rok said – it was just that, the previous year, they'd had another rider from a different team, Steven Kruijswijk from LottoNL–Jumbo, join up on some of their rides … and a month or so later Kruijswijk was one of their main rivals on GC at the Tour. Confused, I made the point to Rok that INEOS didn't have a sprinter, and Dimension Data didn't have a GC rider, lest they be concerned about me 'robbing' any training secrets. There was nothing he could do, Rok said. This was the order from the top.

None of it made any sense … until another INEOS rider, the Dutchman Dylan van Baarle, showed up. I didn't like Dylan and he didn't like me. We'd 'met' at the 2016 Tour de France – a tangle mid-stage when I was in the yellow jersey, followed by an angry exchange of views. Since then we'd had nothing to do with each other. Not a word. Just studious avoidance. Later, much later, I'd discover that it was not a management decision to 'ban' me from the rides at Isola 2000. It doesn't take a genius … Dylan and I also now get on fine. But at the time, suddenly, I was isolated again, seeing the INEOS guys go one way in the morning and having to diplomatically head off in the opposite direction. Then grinding over mountains on my own for the next several hours. At one point I think Luke took pity on me and organised for Peta to come to surprise me. She stayed a couple of days, which gave me a lift. Then it was back to my solo Sherpa expeditions.

I'd not done a lot of altitude training before but thought I'd learned enough to know the formula that worked for most people. It consisted of a long block like the one I'd just done, then a stage race in which I'd usually lack speed and zip, followed by a shorter top-up at altitude. Here, this time, the race would be the Tour of Slovenia in June, which I finished winless but feeling strong, especially on the last stage. From Slovenia I then took my mate Bernie Eisel's advice and made the short journey to a hotel in the mountains above where he lived in Austria. The view is frozen in my mind's eye – both of the glistening, snow-capped peaks through my bedroom window and of the wood-panelled interior of what, in the blink of an eye and bleep of my phone, became a torture chamber, a new mental prison. Another text message. This time: 'You haven't been selected for the Tour.'

The decision had apparently been made in a very long conference call between the main 'brains' in management. Rolf had forcefully argued that my form and prep were on track, Spindler concurred, but others in the room, and particularly Doug Ryder and one of the team's coaches, Daniel Green, didn't agree. It finally went to a vote, with the majority deciding I shouldn't be selected. This despite a couple of the people present calling Rolf a few minutes after the call had ended to say they already regretted voting against me. The question of who would replace me, Rolf told me later, seemed less important than making sure I wasn't going. The team had struggled all year, so they weren't exactly spoiled for choice. They asked a climber who had broken his wrist in the middle of May, Louis Meintjes, but he declined; his hand was still in plaster. In the end, they took Lars Bak, who hadn't even been on the long list. It was evidently a case of 'anyone but Cavendish'.

I was in disbelief. Perhaps naively, I hadn't even considered the possibility that I wouldn't be going to the Tour. Everything I'd done over the previous few months had been geared towards this. Now I headed back to the UK and tried, at least, to take the moral high ground. It seemed there were people in the team who wanted to break me; I showed them they couldn't by playing the model team-mate, even from afar, sending our Italian sprinter, Giacomo Nizzolo, my congratulations and advice on how to approach the first few stages. He did his best and started with a fourth place but never came close to winning again, and eventually abandoned the Tour on stage 12.

That summer and the rest of that year ended up being another blur. I was back to 'just' existing – in a state of numb disassociation from my body, my mind, my present and my future. I wallowed in self-pity, blaming friends, enemies, sometimes even family and, yes, Peter Sagan for that crash in 2017 that had changed everything. It had 'ruined my life', was how I would explain and contextualise it to anyone who listened.

For years Sagan and I simply didn't speak. His team at the time of the crash, BORA–hansgrohe, immediately tried to get his disqualification from the Tour overturned, failed, but responded to that by bringing a legal case against the UCI with the Court of Arbitration for Sport. Just before the first hearing, BORA dropped the case when the UCI accepted that the crash had been 'unfortunate and unintentional' and, hence, Peter should have been allowed to stay in the Tour. I obviously took this badly, as them pointing the finger of blame at me, or at least emboldening the legions of trolls on social media who had done exactly that at the time.

Time is a great healer but my resentment towards Sagan didn't ease. In 2018 our paths barely crossed but when they did I avoided eye contact. In races, I also gave him a wide berth, except for one stage of the 2018 Tour that took in some of the infamous cobbled sections of the Paris–Roubaix one-day race, where I witnessed something I'd never seen before and didn't think I ever would: my team-mate Edvald

Boasson Hagen losing his rag, because Sagan had pushed him off the road and into the grass. When Edvald showered him with assorted rebukes, and I joined in, Sagan just shrugged, grunted back and melted into the middle of the peloton.

They were the last words we 'exchanged' for over a year. Then, one day at the Tour of California in 2019, he tentatively approached me behind the podium. His tone and body language were conciliatory, rather than defiant. But I just glared at him. Sagan's manager, the former sprinter Giovanni Lombardi, quickly stepped in to try to mediate, but I also gave Giovanni short shrift. That crash had 'ruined my life', I snapped at Giovanni. I didn't care that it was BORA making the legal threats and not Peter, I said. They'd also undermined the commissaires as individuals and, as far as I was concerned, in doing so, the whole sport and how it was officiated.

Over the two or three years that followed there was no sign of any 'rapprochement'. If my antipathy flared less often, it was because Sagan was also fading into his twilight years as a rider. His achievements and status of one of the most popular riders of our generation nonetheless remained – which is why, in 2023, Tour organisers A.S.O. wanted him and me to take part in a pair of exhibition races they arranged at the end of every season to promote the Tour in the Far East. Not only that, but for that year's race in Singapore, they wanted

Sagan and me to ride together, as allies, in the same 'Allstars' or 'Legends' team.

The first I heard of this was when I read about the line-up in the cycling media. And I was not amused. 'No fucking way! Not happening. I can't even be in the same room as the guy …' I told A.S.O.'s booker, Vincent Wathelet, in a phone call. I forget how the rest of the conversation went, but Vincent is a master diplomat; he must be, because, somehow, a few days later, I was flying to Singapore to ride in a bike race with Peter Sagan as my team-mate.

From there the 'ceasefire' happened in stages. Act one was monosyllabic but civil conversation in the 'paddock' before the race in Singapore, mainly to discuss tactics. Act two was a surprisingly harmonious and enjoyable team effort in the race. Act three took place that evening – a chat in the famous rooftop bar at the Marina Bay Sands hotel, starting with small talk and eventually broaching 2017 and our relationship since that day. Not everything was settled and agreed upon, but we'd found enough common ground for Gabriele Uboldi, Sagan's PR guy, to suggest that we carry on the conversation over dinner before A.S.O.'s next criterium in Saitama in Japan in a few days' time.

Peta had joined me in Japan, which made it a table for four. Again, I was surprised by how much Sagan and I agreed upon. Not necessarily about the crash itself but the aftermath, and how we'd both seen cycling change over the years. I also got a sense for some of the challenges he'd had in his career, and for how much or little he knew about certain decisions taken on his behalf. Peta is an incredible listener, a master at putting people at ease, and I could see Peter opening up. When dinner ended, we decamped to a tiny, dimly lit whisky bar in the backstreets of Saitama. We stayed there sipping gin and tonics and chatting until four in the morning.

So it was that the 'rift' was healed in a way I never could have contemplated or, until that point, entertained: simply by us talking. I'd suddenly got closure in the sense that my bitterness towards Sagan had been completely neutralised by a bit of mutual empathy – the act of sitting opposite each other, looking into each other's eyes, laughing together and feeling each other's pain. In my case, the previous six years had been wracked with anguish and confusion – but I could also now fully appreciate how that day, 5 July 2017, and its repercussions, had become the through-line in everything that had occurred since. If I was still racing in 2023, it was for three reasons: my legacy in the sport, securing my family's future and – maybe the most viscerally affecting of the lot – my determination to get back what had been taken from me that afternoon: my career.

The other two, if it had all ended in 2019 or 2020 or even 2022, I could have somehow worked out, but not this. A literal void – in my *palmarès*, in terms of the victories I no doubt gave up – would remain, and the emotional one would be even greater. The feeling that the story of my life had not only been edited without my consent but, even worse, no longer even made sense, despite everyone rushing to offer their interpretations. 'He lost it …' 'He got too old …' 'He lost the hunger …' etc. etc. etc. I'd heard them all since 2017. The only way to set the record straight was to write an ending that satisfied me.

I was old and realistic enough by now to know that it wouldn't necessarily be the fairytale finale of a thirty-fifth Tour stage win. Even what had seemed like a 'miracle' – my phoenix-from-the-ashes return to the Tour de France and four stage wins in 2021 – had partially obscured the inconvenient truth that my mental health hadn't been fully, magically restored. The reality was that leaving Dimension Data and removing myself from what to me had become negative influences kick-started a process of realignment – but there was no sudden epiphany or rebirth. Yes, at Bahrain–McLaren in 2020, while I may not have found great success, I did find personalities who helped to lift me – for example, Heinrich Haussler, Marcel Sieberg and Fred Wright. It was true also that, the next year at Soudal–QuickStep, I was surrounded by even more of those, as well as a level of faith that unlocked abilities most people assumed I'd lost. And, yes, it would be accurate to say that as I improved physically my mood and self-esteem also improved.

As much as I hate to break the news, though … I still felt that something inside me had broken or wouldn't come back after 2017: some of the *connectedness* I used to feel – to myself, my emotions, my life. David Spindler had helped me in 2019 primarily by making me feel supported, listened to and represented in an environment where, for a long time, my overwhelming sense had been one of abandonment. But I'd undergone no transformational process of therapy or treatment, or even happened upon a quick-fix hack that I could spin as an inspirational message. If I had one of those, it was that you should never give up or accept someone else dictating when you *should*, indeed, give up … but that didn't mean persistence would necessarily result in the dream outcome. I had the perfect family, assured status among the legends of my sport, wealth and my physical health. And yet – several years later, after 'one of the greatest sporting comebacks ever' and even a Netflix documentary celebrating my mental health journey – there was no neat, perfectly tied bow on any of it. I was still searching, still struggling, with no guarantee of when or even if that would end.

CHAPTER 4

I f receiving my non-summons to the 2019 Tour had felt like being blindsided by a knockout punch, receiving confirmation that I wasn't in QuickStep's final eight for 2022 was like watching my opponent wind up in slow motion, seeing the inevitable hit coming but finding my feet frozen to the canvas.

I'd held out hope until the very last. Traditionally teams announce their final line-ups on the Monday or Tuesday before the Tour, after the National Road Race Championships which give a final meter-reading of form and preparedness. In 2022, the British Nationals were taking place in Castle Douglas in Cumbria. I arrived with my own mini-support team of my eldest son, Finn; a mechanic from QuickStep, Kenny Latomme; and one of the team's soigneurs, David Geeroms. On the afternoon before the race, I lay on David's massage table and told him: 'You watch, tomorrow I'm either going to destroy everyone else from the beginning of the race, or I'm going to implode myself. I'm going all in. Win or bust.'

I woke the next morning to pouring rain and a flutter of excitement as I looked out the window. I'd been here countless times before – at the start of a bike race, surrounded by riders huddled in their rain jackets, looking glumly at the dark clouds overhead, already mentally beaten. Years earlier, Roger Hammond, a three-time national champion, had also let me in on the secrets of doing well in this race, regardless of the year or the course. With everyone representing their own 'trade team' and a field made up of WorldTour pros and domestic part-timers, the racing didn't follow the same rhythms and choreography that were hardwired into every WorldTour rider's subconscious. The UK roads were coarse, 'grippy' – hence the bike didn't 'flow' and neither did the racing. It was stop-start, jerky, one long barrage of attacks and counterattacks.

In my first few years of riding the Nationals I hadn't necessarily taken Roger's advice, but finally the penny had dropped when I took my first win in 2013. Now, nine years on, in 2022, I rode like a bully, teasing and brutalising my rivals before eventually winning a three-man sprint for the title. To the pride of pulling on the national champion's jersey for a second time was added the satisfaction of demonstrating that I was also in a 'proper' bike race. Bunch sprints were not the only domain in which I could hold my own; they were just the arena in which I could most excel relative to the best bike riders in the world.

I'd done all that I could. At least now no one could say I didn't deserve to be in the Tour team, simply hadn't got the form or had gone on for one season too long. Patrick himself messaged to say that I'd amazed him yet again, that I never stopped amazing him. This was a couple of hours before the team sent out a press release announcing their team for the Tour. I was on it as one of two reserves, along with Florian Sénéchal, who'd just become national champion of France.

The statement quoted Tom Steels: 'Fabio has proved how fast and strong he is in the sprints and will now get to discover Le Tour … Concerning our reserves, we must stress out that they showed a lot of professionalism, continued to train and remained focused in these past couple of weeks, and even brought two victories at the Nationals.'

In other words, I'd be spending July at home, unless one of the anointed eight got ill or injured in the next four days.

Only a few hours later the team sent out another communiqué: one of the original eight picks, Tim Declercq, had indeed gone down with Covid. He'd be replaced by Florian Sénéchal.

All I could do was shrug and wish the lads the best. In fairness, they also had an incredible start to the Tour, with Yves Lampaert causing a massive upset and taking the first stage and yellow jersey in Copenhagen. Fabio then took his first stage win the following day. At the time of writing, four years on, it was also his last.

At least now there could be no ambiguity about my future with QuickStep – or rather lack thereof. I'd also started to weigh up my alternatives from some time in the spring. My coach, Vasi, knew that I was 'on the market', which was why, during our training camp in Greece in the spring, he wanted me to meet an old friend of his, an agent, over dinner one night in Athens. The guy's name was Martijn Berkhout. He worked for an agency, SEG, which also had an academy team that Vasi used to coach. As we ate, Martijn quickly cut to the chase: he knew how much, or rather how little, I was earning, and he thought it was a travesty. It was also inexplicable to him that we were in April and I hadn't even started fielding offers from other teams for the following season. He asked if I had an agent, to which I replied that I had a manager for off-the-bike contracts, but that I'd generally negotiated my own deals with teams. I didn't give away my trust easily, I said. Maybe I had control issues. In this case, if he could get me two respectable offers for 2023, he could have my custom and my commission. He said that we had a deal.

Throughout the rest of the spring and during the Tour, Martijn worked hard to find me a new home. Finally, he said he'd got an interesting, if slightly left-field option for me: an old team-mate of mine, the Frenchman Jérôme Pineau, was upscaling his second-tier team, B&B Hotels, and wanted me to be his 'franchise player', his star signing. Jérôme had been a decent rider, not a superstar but one of the stronger French guys of his generation, and as team-mates we'd always got on. He was outspoken – highly quotable and oft-quoted, including on controversial topics like doping. Early in his career he'd railed against dope-cheats in the media – but he was also a staunch defender of anyone who was being baselessly accused. In the seasons he'd spent riding in a 'foreign' team, QuickStep, he'd seen from a distance how French teams' disgruntlement with their own lack of success had spawned a jealousy and paranoia that everyone who was winning *must* be cheating, *bien sûr*. In 2021, when I came back from oblivion, I'd been the target of some of this – murmurs and mumbles that it was 'impossible', a Cinderella story that must also be a fairytale – and Jérôme had set the doubters straight. You don't know him, Jérôme had told them. Look at what he's done. Look at the rest of his career. I know him, you don't, he'd said. I'd appreciated that immensely.

The idea of riding for someone who would back and stick up for me was highly appealing. Throughout my career I've used critics and sceptics and their lack of faith as fuel, but within my circle, my tribe, I run on belief and confidence. I said it years ago about one of my first coaches, the Australian Shane Sutton: others found him abrasive, but he worked for me because, to put it in the sort of terms he would employ, he blew the right amount of sunshine up my arse. Jérôme could tick that box, and his project sounded exciting … but, equally, I had reservations. First and foremost: the similarity with Dimension Data. There, too, I'd joined a team which wanted to elevate its status by standing on my shoulders. This was the way teams often grew – in fact there weren't many other ways you could do it – but there were also inherent dangers. Often, the superior talent was simply bolted on to what had been and remained a B-standard team in every other respect, from the riders who ended up becoming your domestiques to the operational processes and backroom staff. As the franchise player, the would-be saviour, you could also end up under inordinate amounts of pressure to deliver, as had been the case with me at Dimension Data. There, too, Doug Ryder had evidently had faith initially. It simply turned to toilet paper as soon as I started to struggle for reasons beyond my control, the other riders couldn't step up either and sponsors started getting twitchy.

Another issue with teams trying to step up to the next level is that the plan is often tied to an investment that isn't yet signed, sealed and delivered. Over the years there have been innumerable teams and managers who have talked publicly or privately about massive new injections of cash, only for those never to materialise. Often an almost inescapable Catch-22 is created – the prospective sponsor won't pony up until a star rider has signed on, but, equally, the star rider doesn't want to commit until he's sure the money's in place. Jérôme couldn't say too much about where his windfall was supposedly coming from, but it was pretty widely reported that the Council of Paris and tourist board were involved. The Olympics were coming in 2024, and a professional cycling team would be part of the legacy plan.

I trusted Jérôme. Financially, I thought we could also come to an agreement. Equally, though, the idea of signing for an established, top-tier team felt like a safer bet. Martijn also informed me that he knew of two that were interested: EF Education–EasyPost and Israel–Premier Tech. The former was run by a preppy, slightly eccentric and awkward ex-rider from Colorado named Jonathan Vaughters, who wasn't everyone's cup of root beer and might not ordinarily have been mine. His team also didn't have a history of supporting sprinters, which added to my scepticism. Nevertheless, EF, whose main business is language schools, seemed a good company. I also gathered that a clothing company, Rapha, and a bike supplier, Cannondale, were keen to have me … And so a call was set up between me and JV. It turned out to be friendly, broadly constructive and encouraging, and I was keeping an open mind, but we left it that JV would get back in touch with what he could offer. Fine, I said. We'd speak soon.

At this point, for context, I need to go back in time, to say that I had nearly joined JV's team once before, right at the start of my career and their existence. I'd signed my first pro deal ahead of the 2007 season with T-Mobile, the German team I'd dreamed of joining ever since my early teens. The terms: two years at €45,000 a year. It was a decent amount, especially for a 21-year-old rookie who wouldn't be expected to deliver much in the way of results in his first season. I had no idea at that point whether I was going to cut it as a pro, either ... but that quickly changed when I got my first race win in the April, then my second and third in the May, and my fourth and fifth in the June. Within the space of two-and-a-bit months, I'd become the hottest young property in the sport, a wanted man. So coveted, in fact, that Dave Millar, who was riding for Vaughters's Garmin team, pulled me aside one day at the Volta a Catalunya in May to tell me that Jonathan wanted to sign me. I was so coveted that Jonathan's price, when Dave then introduced us in a team bus car park the following day, was €250,000 a season.

In my naivety, I decided there and then that I would simply inform my T-Mobile team manager, Bob Stapleton, that I wanted out of my contract. Of course it wasn't that simple – the deal couldn't just be broken, plus Bob and JV's relationship was increasingly antagonistic, a simmering rivalry that over the next couple of years would turn quite spicy. Hence, Bob put his foot down, while also making a counterproposal: the same wage that JV was offering, but for three more seasons. I agreed on the spot. In fact without checking whether the new terms kicked in immediately, or at the end of the year, which turned out to be the case. So, per the new contract, I'd be paid €250,000 a year in 2008, 2009 and 2010.

Again, these figures are important, because consider now that, when JV's offer dropped into my inbox in the late summer of 2022 – that's to say 15 years and 160 race wins later – it was for €150,000, a little more than half of what he'd offered me in 2007. That's without even taking inflation into account.

Don't get me wrong, I know that a lot of people living in the UK and other parts of the world would kill to be on that kind of money, but, in the circumstances, it was a clear statement to me that JV wasn't interested. He was wasting my time. Pretending to be interested because his sponsors were. I don't think I even replied.

Next up, Martijn said, were Israel–Premier Tech. They were an interesting one because they'd gained a reputation as a sort of lucrative 'retirement home' for ageing stars. This was partly but not entirely based on the reportedly astronomical deal they'd done for my mate Chris Froome when he left Team Sky at the end of 2020. Froomey was struggling to regain top form after his almost career-ending crash at the Critérium du Dauphiné in 2019, but Israel's team owner, a rich and larger-than-life Canadian-Israeli businessman called Sylvan Adams, had gambled that he would by offering him a massive, five-year contract. Let's just say that it hadn't exactly panned out on the road, not through any lack of effort or endeavour on Froomey's part.

I knew Adams would probably offer decent money. They needed results, a proven winner. I also knew and had a positive impression of Rob Gitelis, the CEO of Factor Bikes, Israel's bike supplier. He, like Sylvan, was keen to have me on the team. This had made Sylvan even more enthusiastic. We arranged a call for the last week of September.

Unfortunately, after the chat, I was less enthused. Sylvan spent most of the call warning me about B&B, as far as I could tell regurgitating rumours that had started to make it into the press about the solidity of that team's new investment. He then followed up with a long text message repeating a lot of what he'd said – including a short lecture about French tax laws, and how I'd end up paying more on a French team. I of course knew this already. I'd been more curious to hear about Sylvan's team, their ambitions. But on that topic he seemed a lot less animated and loquacious. In relation to his own team, he'd mainly wanted to emphasise one thing: their budget constraints. It didn't fill me with great confidence or hope.

We'd agreed to speak again the following day, but before then I got another call, this one from Sylvan's team manager, a Belgian ex-rider named Rik Verbrugghe. Again, this was pleasant enough but I didn't feel inspired. It had also started to feel a bit like a three-line whip.

The specifics hadn't yet been discussed, but Sylvan was about to get to that. He said that he could offer me a €500,000 salary and a €1 million bonus if I won a stage at the Tour, number 35. He was clearly treating it like a big gamble, a high-stakes bet … which I didn't particularly like, either. I'd guess that 100 riders in the pro peloton earn in excess of €1 million a season, despite rarely winning or being recognised outside their home country or in some cases home city. Jérôme's whole pitch had been that of someone who wanted to invest, not take a wild punt. I told Sylvan I'd prefer a €1 million salary and no bonus, not because I didn't think I'd get the Tour stage, or because I desperately wanted or needed that guaranteed money, but because of what that said about his faith in me. I could appreciate that he felt burned by Froomey's deal, but it didn't sit right that he only seemed to want me on the proviso that I could hit the jackpot of a thirty-fifth stage. Because – as I'd explain to him – my ability to do that also depended largely on him and the team he put around me. It was all too reminiscent of Dimension Data, and so I told him 'thank you', I'd appreciated his interest, but I'd rather take my chances elsewhere.

So that was that. From three 'options', we were down to one: Jérôme and B&B. It was now early October, later than you'd expect a project like this to be unveiled, but Jérôme assured me that all was in hand. The team already existed, of course, but they, we, would be making a big step up, with a whole new cohort of established riders joining. One of the most experienced lead-out men in the business, the Argentine Max Richeze, would be coming from the UAE team, on my recommendation, and we'd also have two Dutchmen,

Cees Bol and Ramon Sinkeldam, both of whom knew their way around a sprint finish. The women's team was also shaping up, with the French national time-trial champion, Audrey Cordon-Ragot, top of the bill. It all sounded exciting and, above all, convincing. Rumours were still swirling about budget shortfalls, delays, maybe the money not even being there. I felt secure to the extent that I'd downloaded Duolingo and was brushing up my schoolboy French.

The terms were all agreed, a letter of intent finally signed. We, the riders, were then summoned to a meeting near Paris to get fitted for kit and our bikes, which were to be supplied by the Swiss manufacturer BMC. The last pieces of the jigsaw, Jérôme said, would be in place in time for the 2023 Tour de France route presentation. That would be held, like every year, at the end of October in Paris, so was the perfect occasion to officially 'launch' the 'new' team, which of course had the official backing of the Council of Paris. What we didn't know at the time, but was reported later, was that Paris had never intended to put in any money; at one point there'd been talk of €10 million, but the deal that actually got signed, on the last day of the 2022 Tour de France, was for a logo on the jersey, the sheer prestige and pulling power of being associated with Paris, and nothing else.

On 17 October, the French press confirmed what they'd been hinting at for a while: Mark Cavendish would sign for B&B Hotels. The grand unveiling would take place at a press conference the day before the Tour presentation. So they reported, but it turned out to be fake news, because three or four days later Jérôme messaged everyone to say that there was a small hiccup, nothing fatal but serious enough, nonetheless, to force a postponement.

This was now awkward. I'd be attending the Tour presentation, as would lots of journalists. They'd want answers. Audrey Cordon-Ragot came rushing over as soon as she spotted me in the auditorium. She thought we were being taken for a ride, that Jérôme had oversold his hand. I tried to reassure her: he was a good guy, I knew he'd be doing everything he could. I said that if and when we were asked about the team, we should just steer the conversation straight back to the Tour or the Tour de France Femmes. Which is exactly what I ended up doing, not that it wasn't embarrassing and, frankly, a bit suspicious.

October melted into November. The deadline for team registration and bank guarantees to be filed with the UCI had come and gone, but Jérôme had secured an extension. In mid-November he was still telling the press that he had five potential sponsors, and two weeks to get one or more of them signed up. I, though, was now resigned to looking elsewhere, in a desert of options, way past the date when most teams had finalised their 2023 rosters. It might take something unorthodox – which Martijn Berkhout told me he may have found with an existing American team called

Human Powered Health. Currently, they raced at a similar level to B&B, but they too were interested in going to the next level. Their bike sponsor, Felt, was particularly keen on me acting as their game changer.

Felt were part of larger group, Pierer Mobility, with a huge presence in the motorcycle world. I know them and their brands well thanks partly to my friendship with Cal Crutchlow, the MotoGP rider. Now, with Jérôme's B&B dream looking dead in the water, Felt invited me to the Pierer headquarters in Austria to get to know the company and what they had in mind with Human Powered Health. I ended up going and being blown away. Their ambition was huge, as were their resources. There was also no sense of them hedging their bets, no belittling of other teams or organisations, nothing that tripped my bullshit alarm. They knew it would be hard, if not impossible, to get invited to the Tour in 2023, with the current Human Powered Health roster plus me and a few other 'survivors' of the B&B fiasco. But they weren't fazed. They were ready to go all in. Whatever it took.

I left Austria buzzing but still unsure. Pierer's 'can do' mentality wasn't quite matched by the existing management at Human Powered Health. I'd told them that with just me we'd struggle to get a slot in the 2023 Tour, that to be sure we needed something big. I suggested buying my QuickStep team-mate, Julian Alaphilippe, out of his contract, given that he and Patrick Lefevere were on the rocks. I still also wanted

Max Richeze as my lead-out man. Here, they started to baulk. Richeze had tested positive for a steroid at the start of his career; he'd been cleared by his national federation but was still banned on appeal. They didn't want him and didn't see the Alaphilippe idea as realistic or even necessary. My impression was that they underestimated the difficulty of the Tour and what it would take to win there.

My issue now was that there were no 'good' options. We were entering 'beggars can't be choosers' territory.

Mid-December. We were now a month from the Tour Down Under, the first WorldTour race of the season. Jérôme had also messaged everyone to say, with regret, that there would definitely be no team. I'd figured that out already, but what now? At times like this, with questions like the ones I now faced, I always tried to order my thoughts and feelings by writing them down. At any one time I'll have several notebooks on the go – always in my suitcase at races, or somewhere safe at home – that I fill with ideas, doodles or, if I have a decision to make, lists of pros and cons. As soon as I'd known I wouldn't be staying with QuickStep, earlier in 2022, I'd started jotting down the names of teams who I thought could be interested, and the perks and drawbacks of each one. I now went back to look at what I'd written …

'Teams: EF, Trek, BORA, Alpecin, B&B …'

And at some of the things I'd written underneath.

'BORA: plus, I know management and riders, good lead-out, Specialized bikes, functional Germans; minus, might be changing bikes, GC focus …'

'Alpecin: plus, like a watered-down QuickStep, stage-win focused, good equipment, racing team, flexibility with image rights; minus, they've got two other sprinters in Philipsen and Groves, no post-career opportunities …

'EF: plus, great partners for your IP and collaborations, definite Tour place, marketable team, know enough people to settle in; minus, performance question marks, some equipment not great, JV …'

Some of these were pure ideas that had come to nothing. Others had been overtaken by events – for example EF's miserly offer, and the fact that nothing had materialised from Alpecin despite a reasonably positive Zoom call with their owners, the Roodhooft brothers. Martijn had also got a no from Lidl–Trek. Arkéa–Samsic: No. TotalEnergies also gave me short shrift. Theirs had been the logo on my first ever racing jersey, when I was a kid in the Isle of Man. But neither this nor the fact that Peter Sagan was retiring and taking his wage off their books made any difference; it was a firm '*Non!*'

What had remained evergreen was my pyramid or hierarchy of my priorities. Now, in December, with next to nothing on the horizon, I read those back:

1. Be HAPPY. Environment. People.
2. PERFORM (team, riders, staff, equipment).
3. Fair pay – not to be rich, just to be compensated for my work.
4. Marketability: IP freedom, brands, marketing.
5. Post-career: don't need anything concrete but want options.

And underneath all that, a line that had been a constant refrain in my inner monologue for months, if not years: 'Important to utilise these last years to set up post-career. WIN. Don't fizzle out.'

All of this was written down with the intention of making decisions easier – but, as things stood, there was no decision to make. No doors left to knock. I'd exhausted the offbeat options and the obvious. Even the very obvious. Including the most obvious.

CHAPTER 5

As of December 2022, there was one 'British' team in elite professional cycling. That had indeed been the case for most of my career: when I turned pro in 2007, the UK was to road cycling roughly what sub-Saharan Africa is to alpine skiing – just two British riders having lined up in the previous year's Tour de France, after a 2005 edition where there were none. That of course was all about to change spectacularly with my generation, ourselves the product of a grand, lottery-funded plan drawn up years earlier, which would culminate with the creation of Team Sky in 2010. A UK team had last competed in the Tour in the 1980s, but Sky and the main brain behind the team, Dave Brailsford, had a much bigger ambition than that: the first ever British victory in the Tour – British rider, British team – within five years. It ended up taking them two: Sir Bradley Wiggins became the first man to walk on the Moon, in cycling terms, in 2012.

Five more British Tour wins later, Sky had become INEOS in 2019. That was also the year of their most recent Tour de France win, with the Colombian Egan Bernal. Since then cycling had changed, racing become more explosive, evolved away from the hyper-controlled Brailsford blueprint, and there was a feeling that INEOS's identity was also very different from Sky's. 'Dave B' himself had been commandeered to INEOS's multidisciplinary 'mission' to dominate various sports, not just cycling. Dave had handed the keys to his old kingdom to Rod Ellingworth – this after a falling out in 2019, when Rod left for the Bahrain team, only for Dave to bring him back a year later to essentially do Dave's old job.

Of course, my relationship with Rod had also had its ups and downs. Or at least one big down. That had come at the end of my one and only season at Bahrain, in 2020. I'd been led to believe there would be a second, and maybe even a future off the bike beyond that, but the team decided otherwise. I'd hoped he'd fight my corner … Up to that point Rod had been probably the single biggest positive influence on my career: the man who, as I once said in a newspaper interview, had turned me from 'a fat banker into a world-class cyclist' – he picked me for the British Cycling Academy's inaugural intake in 2004, gave me the tools to turn pro, and thereby saved me from my previous job as a cashier at Barclays bank in Douglas. But then, by showing me no faith when I most needed it, at one of the lowest ebbs of my career, Rod had misjudged and deserted me. At least that's how I'd felt at the time.

Over the next few months we didn't speak. I'd see him at races and either carry straight on or barely acknowledge him with a nod or grunt. The anger eventually dissipated but I couldn't help feeling hurt. In cycling, though, there are some people with whom you've shared too much and too rich of a journey for it all to be erased. Time eventually healed the wound. He'd done a lot for me. Perhaps he'd also been fearing for his own future at Bahrain. Consequently, earlier in the summer of 2022, when I'd initially texted Brailsford to ask whether INEOS may be interested, and he told me to ask Rod, I did it without feeling particularly awkward or embarrassed. He also didn't seem sheepish in any way, although he couldn't offer me my fairytale ending either: INEOS had one sprinter, Elia Viviani, and were otherwise mainly focused on regaining their status as the top dogs in Grand Tours.

So that was that. Until the end of November when, with the B&B ship now sunk, I got a call from Rod. They were working on something. Something that would blow the budget and a bit more. But it may not come off. And if it didn't, there might be a place at INEOS.

I didn't need Rod to tell me that the 'something big' was signing Remco Evenepoel. After Pogačar, the Belgian was the latest wunderkind on the international cycling scene, and INEOS were desperate to buy him out of his contract with QuickStep. This sort of deal was rare in cycling because it was complex and expensive. Knowing my soon-to-be-old

QuickStep boss Patrick Lefevere, who'd have to give his blessing, it looked like a long shot ... but in cycling, like everywhere else, money talked.

The question then would be: did I want to go to INEOS? It was reasonable to ask, not so much because of what had gone on between Rod and me at Bahrain, but because of what had happened with me and Sky. When I signed for them in 2012, I was one half of a British dream ticket, with Sir Bradley Wiggins. We duly delivered a Tour de France that surpassed and eclipsed even Brailsford's wildest patriotic dreams, with Brad riding into Paris in the yellow jersey ... and me riding off his wheel, in the world champion's rainbow bands, to take my third stage win of that year's race on the Champs-Elysées. A decade on I still had no hesitation in calling it the greatest moment of my career. But it was also the last time I would ride for Sky at the Tour, because we parted ways at the end of the season two years before my contract was due to expire. It was very simple: they were a GC team, I was a sprinter.

Ten-plus years later there was evidence everywhere of innovations that they, or we, brought to the sport. Sadly, after Sky's departure and INEOS's arrival, there was also evidence of a clear regression in the popularity of pro cycling in the UK, some of it down to the force majeure of other nations and their riders emerging to take centre stage, some of it reflecting more on the void that Sky and their marketing juggernaut had left.

Anyhow, it was a decade since my uncoupling from the only British team to compete at the highest level of the sport during my career, and now here I was, wondering whether we could reconcile for an unlikely swansong. Rod had said that he would know 'in a few days', but I was getting anxious, so I suggested expediting things: how about I sent a presentation or deck to him and Dave Brailsford? Rod confirmed that it would be Dave who would have the ultimate say, so I should send it to him. 'I can't stop thinking about this now,' I said to Rod in a message. 'It just feels right for me and the team.'

A few days later the PDF landed in Dave Brailsford's inbox. With it, I sent a few words explaining that, if INEOS clearly had a contender to win the Tour de France, I wouldn't be wasting my time or Dave's, but, in the absence of that, I could be the next best thing. Over nine slides, the pitch document spelled out how and why.

- How it'd bring my relationship with British Cycling, the organisation that had given birth to Team Sky, full circle.
- How me winning a thirty-fifth Tour stage would sit perfectly alongside the other record and paradigm-breaking feats which INEOS and their sports-mad owner Sir Jim Ratcliffe were sponsoring, from Eliud Kipchoge's sub-two-hour marathon to Ben Ainslie's Americas Cup bid; from Lewis Hamilton's final push

to be universally recognised as the greatest ever F1 driver with the Mercedes team to the All Blacks continued domination of international rugby.

- Why a 2023 Tour de France route that was one of the most mountainous in recent memory would play in our favour – because every other team would double down on climbing talent.
- Why, at 37, I still had what it took to both succeed myself and elevate the level of the team, particularly the next generation.
- How even leaving the Tour and what I could do in the saddle to one side, the story alone was irresistible, inspiring and commercially compelling.

It took me almost a week to put together. It took Brailsford the same time to respond, though via Rod. The answer, in summary: no thanks, Cav. INEOS Grenadiers weren't signing Mark Cavendish … and they didn't sign Remco Evenepoel.

· · ·

Christmas was approaching but, as far as my career was concerned, there was no sign of Santa and his sleigh. 'No room at the inn' was the message I'd been hearing for weeks. That, though, was about to change. One day in December, I was out shopping for Peta's birthday present when I got a call from my old friend called Vincent Wathelet. Belgian, probably in his mid-sixties although I'd feel rude asking, larger than life, Vincent is one of those ubiquitous, almost universally appreciated institutions in the cycling world that everyone knows … without knowing exactly how they know him or what he does. A cycling nut from birth, later a team manager, then a rider agent and TV producer, he'd performed as many different roles as he'd seen generations come and go. He'd been called many things, including 'wheeler-dealer', but he was above all a true, dyed-in-the-wool lover of professional cycling and its people – *his* people, *his* tribe.

I'd always liked Vincent but he wasn't a regular caller, so I was immediately curious. And he got pretty much straight to the point.

'Hello, Mark. How are you? I am at dinner with someone who wants to talk to you. I'm giving him the phone now …'

I recognised the next voice I heard immediately: Alexander Vinokourov, the long-time manager of the Astana team. In truth, I'd also known for a couple of months that they might be interested in signing me. I certainly knew that Vinokourov and Martijn Berkhout had had a conversation. Frankly, though, it was not an option that I'd taken seriously, mainly because of the team's complete lack of pedigree when it came to sprinting – which looked to me like a clear reflection of Vinokourov's own feelings about that particular sub-discipline of professional cycling: he simply wasn't interested. His team had won the Tour de France, the Giro d'Italia and Vuelta a España, and, even in their leaner years, had survived as a sanctuary for mountain goats.

In his own racing career, although built more like a honey badger, Vino had excelled when going uphill to the extent that had won a Vuelta overall and Tour stages in the Alps. It said it all that, over the previous quarter of a century, one man had managed to ruin the sprinters' biggest occasion of the season – the annual sprint on the Champs-Elysées in the Tour de France – and that had been Vino, when he powered clear, on his own, from a very embarrassed peloton in the last kilometres in 2005.

And yet now that guy was telling me that I would make history on Champs, with his team, the following July.

I'm sure I immediately sounded sceptical. But he assured me he was serious. Astana didn't have another star and had also lost some of their old identity, as the marauding stage-hunters of the Alps and Pyrenees. I asked him about a lead-out train and he said we could build one, with riders I recommended. I asked how we were going to win and he said we'd try our best and if it worked, it worked, and if it didn't, it didn't. I asked about many conflicting personal sponsors and he said we'd work something out there, too. We also discussed money and Vino didn't try to drive down my expectations immediately by pleading poverty. The whole call was oddly, refreshingly and – from my point of view – surprisingly free of caveats, emotional blackmail, or the sense that I was getting my intellectual and financial pants pulled down.

Suddenly I could see possibilities instead of only obstacles. I now had a 'choice', admittedly between two options that were also, to an extent, compromises – Astana and Human Powered Health. That was still a whole lot more palatable than going with my tail between my legs, hands held out, to a team who didn't really want or believe in me but could just about find it in their heart and wallet to rescue me from undignified oblivion.

I was leaning towards Astana but each option felt like a thorny path, and I was walking barefoot. Circumstances had tied my destiny to that of a Dutch rider who'd been earmarked for my lead-out train at B&B, Cees Bol, and he was of the opinion that we should both go to Human Powered Health. They were offering me nearly double the money. There were also other issues with Astana – like the team's well-documented, apparently long-running difficulties with paying on time. Not to mention fairly widespread misgivings about the team rooted, one, in prejudice – because they came from and acted almost as a de facto national team for a country familiar to the masses only as the birthplace of 'Borat' – and, two, because of Vino's complicated reputation. As much as his swashbuckling victories at the Tour de France, a lot of fans remembered him leaving the race in disgrace in 2007, having tested positive for a blood transfusion.

Throughout my career I'd been confronted with the ghosts of cycling's darkest age, either side of the millennium. One of my most important mentors and another near-constant in my career, Rolf Aldag, had been a product of those times, a self-confessed but also very much reformed doper and also, incidentally, a team-mate of Vino's at T-Mobile. I could hardly now baulk at being associated with Vinokourov having for years vouched for and indeed evangelised about Rolf. As for my morals, I wasn't about to compromise or allow those to be polluted, at the age of 37. I knew that there'd be questions if I chose Astana, a snarky comment piece here and there, but I also knew my own mind, my motives and the cultural revolution the sport had undergone vis-à-vis doping. Let's be real: it also wasn't as though, in their desperation to sign me, all 18 WorldTour teams had sent me glossy, 50-page brochures laying out their ethically superior Values Charter. *One* WorldTour team was offering me a contract: Alexander Vinokourov's Astana.

The more I thought about the two roads to my desired destination, the Tour – Astana's maybe a little meandering and rutted, but certified by all maps to exist, against Human Powered Health's, which hadn't progressed past the 'Route Feasibility Study' – the easier the decision became. I broke the good news to Vinokourov in a phone-call just before Christmas, whereupon the planning began immediately: the intricacies of the contract that I would eventually sign, my bike and kit measurements, and when exactly during the forthcoming training camp in Spain I would join up with my new team-mates. At this point nothing had leaked into the press – and indeed wouldn't until, a few days later, I emerged from the arrivals hall at Alicante airport wheeling a bike-box, to be greeted by a turquoise blue Astana team car and, a few paces from that, the vaguely familiar face of a man furtively holding up a mobile photo and taking a picture. Within hours the image had 'found its way' onto social media, to be followed by another of me riding on a team-edition Wilier Triestina bike alongside Cees Bol, who had also signed.

In truth, everything – and not just this impromptu, unofficial unveiling – had happened very fast. Cees and I had come down to dinner on the first evening and immediately been confronted with a team dynamic unlike anything I'd experienced in the previous decade-and-a-half. Over that time, English had gradually but unerringly established itself as the lingua franca of professional cycling, but there was evidently one team that remained a last bastion of multilingualism. That was Astana: at one table, rolling 'r's' ricocheting back and forth between Spanish-speakers like pinballs in an arcade machine; at the next, a choreographed ballet of Italian hand gestures; then the Russian-speakers – inscrutable and, to me, incomprehensible. It was less the United Nations than a global jumble sale.

Where would I fit in? The obvious answer, at first, was with the only native English speaker on the team or in the room, the American Joe Dombrowski. Just a couple of years younger than me, Joe was also a veteran of over a decade in the pro ranks, but there, and with language, you might have thought our common ground would end; on the bike, he was a gangly, opportunistic climber, in some ways a throwback to what Astana had been but didn't necessarily want to remain. Out of the saddle, I didn't know him well, but he'd always struck me and been portrayed in the media as a quirky, bookish type who showed up to races with the quizzical, laidback air of a college undergrad spending his summer holiday in Europe, a few novels in his rucksack, an Interrail pass in hand and a head halfway between the clouds and world domination. Joe had been at the team for a year already but still seemed as spaced out, as disoriented, as I was. It was he who talked Cees and me through some of the, shall we say, more idiosyncratic aspects of the team, like the doctor who didn't speak a word of English, or the team WhatsApp group in which none was written. Most of the time, Joe said, you simply had to guess or just nod and hope for the best. Cees and I got back to the room we were sharing that night, looked at each other and just burst out laughing, half horrified, half amused by what we'd witnessed and what we'd got ourselves into.

It was easy to feel that they were a dysfunctional bunch – as evidenced by the results of the last year: in 2022 they'd won the grand total of five races, making it their worst ever season. Equally, I could see fertile terrain for what I'd always regarded as my biggest, most potent quality: the ability to create and nourish a cohesive, winning group. There were also elements of the culture that, far from being disjointed and old-fashioned, were steeped in the *savoir faire* that had been lost from cycling in my time in the peloton. The predominantly Italian mechanics, for example, had the work

ethic of Stakhanovite labourers and the finesse and dexter-
ity of Renaissance painters. The head mechanic, Gabriele
Tosello, had spent years working for Mario Cipollini, the
greatest sprinter of the generation before mine and a notoriously demanding taskmaster when it came to mechanics
and bikes. Maybe Gabriele had heard the same about me,
or perhaps his methods had simply been honed by all those
years tweaking saddles by a millimetre here, a millimetre
there, or soaking tyres in the milk of goats grazing on a
specific north-facing mountainside in the Peruvian Andes.
I'm exaggerating, but you get the idea ... and I immediately got the identical, red-carpet treatment. It was the
same throughout the staff and particularly among the
Italians, whose devotion to the Catholic faith is a well-worn
stereotype, but whose propensity for hero-worship, in my
experience, is even more committed.

Again, it all made for a strange, almost schizophrenic
amalgam. I'd been in teams, for example QuickStep, where
the breakfast room was like a Babylonian banquet, the tables
laden with Haribo sweets and granola, whereas here it was
best described as ... spartan. Rice cakes, a few apples and off
you trot. At the same time, there was a level of protocol and
formality around aspects of team life that verged on opulence,
like the crisp white uniforms that were de rigueur at your daily
massage. Moments of the day when you felt as though you
were peeking behind the Iron Curtain, followed by moments
when it seemed like you'd time travelled back to ancient Rome.

The bike had been another concern. I'd seen at Bahrain three years earlier that a team could have a good bike, which the Merida was, but that wouldn't necessarily mean it suited my sprinting style. Astana's supplier was an Italian 'heritage' brand called Wilier Triestina, whose frames were glorious – the cycling equivalent of an Armani suit or a Ferragamo sandal – but which I suspected might be an example of style over substance and technology. Fortunately, I was wrong: before my first ride at the Alicante camp, I swung my leg over the top tube, clipped in, started gently pressing the pedals and ... immediately breathed a sigh of relief. If this whole adventure ended in embarrassment and abject failure, it wouldn't be all about the bike.

Much more would depend on my legs, and there, I knew, months of hard work lay ahead. Teamless and directionless, I'd nonetheless trained hard throughout the winter, mainly on an indoor trainer and the Zwift online platform. My target every day was simple – and almost always identical: ride four hours. Often, with team managers phoning to bargain or personal sponsors wanting to know whether I was still a bike rider, I'd be on and off the bike like a kangaroo on a trampoline, taking calls, writing emails. Some days I'd start training at eight in the morning ... and finish at eight in the evening. But I'd always fit in my four hours.

The net result was that, at the Alicante camp in January, I was going surprisingly well. The Astana group rides were different from what I'd experienced before, and again reflected what the team had been and where priorities lay. The pace on the flat was steady, almost languid – whereas every climb became a race. Performance uphill also seemed to be the only fitness marker that impressed the directeurs sportif, most of whom, if they weren't from Italy, had spent most of their racing careers in teams there, weaned on the Giro d'Italia and the cult of the mountains.

Practice made, if not perfect, then at least more upwardly mobile than I ordinarily would be in January and February. At the same time, better climbing generally came at a cost of slower sprinting – so I had to be careful. Threading this needle was complicated by the fact that I could no longer count on Vasi, the coach who had revitalised me at QuickStep. At the end of 2022, upon leaving, my parting request to Patrick Lefevere had been to let me carry on working with Vasi, although he'd still be under contract with Patrick. Patrick had agreed. The problem came when the Astana coaches asked for access to my files on TrainingPeaks, the software almost every pro cyclist and team uses to log and analyse their performance data. I hemmed and hawed for a few days, mindful that the Vasi arrangement could cause issues, but finally they practically cornered me in the hotel lobby one day and announced they were going to walk me through the process of uploading my rides. As it turned out, none of the issues came from them … but the very next day I got a call from Vasi: QuickStep's head coach, Koen Pelgrim, was now aware that the Astana coaches had access to the plans that Vasi was prescribing, and he was afraid they would 'copy' them for other Astana riders. This dismayed but didn't necessarily surprise me, coming from Koen: from the moment we'd met during my first spell at QuickStep, it'd been clear that we had diametrically opposed visions of cycling and training – his, as far as I was concerned, shaped in a lab, measurable in numbers, mine dripping with emotion and guided by instinct. After an initial period of friction, we'd pretty much agreed to disagree and stayed out of each other's way while remaining civil. My second spell at QuickStep wasn't even as diplomatic. After he'd laughed in my face while reviewing my 'numbers' at my first training camp, there wasn't even a need to stay out of each other's way. Given the purported motive, this, now, seemed unnecessarily churlish, an attempt to make sure that if I wasn't going to win for QuickStep, I wasn't going to win at all.

I could bristle all I wanted – he wasn't going to change his mind. So it was about finding an alternative. The compromise that Vasi and I found was that I would broadly rely on the training plans he'd given me over the previous two years, or a simplified menu of roughly similar sessions. To keep it in culinary terms, I'd have no master chef looking over my shoulder, but he'd given me a book of his most basic recipes. My, ahem, interpretation would sometimes lack a bit of flair and finesse – sometimes I'd stir in a bit too much of one ingredient, say 30-second intervals rather than 5-minute efforts. Sometimes I might also 'overcook' a block of work or, conversely, turn down the heat before my form was perfectly *al dente*, that is, I'd do too much or too little. But I'd figure it out through trial and error and, if all else failed, be able to call and discretely get Vasi's input now and again.

My racing programme had been decided in January in a meeting with the directeurs sportif. Here, the Italians held sway, particularly Beppe Martinelli or 'Martino' as he was known to everyone in the team. Now in his mid-sixties, Martino had a thick, raspy, northern Italian accent, a thin and rarely seen smile and the sage-like aura of someone who had won everything in the sport, which he had. His view – and also the strong consensus – was that I should race a predominantly Italian programme up to the Tour de France, including the Giro d'Italia. I could see their logic, but, also, I wasn't naive: the organisers of the Giro and several other Italian races on my provisional calendar, RCS, would be *delighted* to have me on the startlist. They would also show Astana their gratitude. These, shall we say, arrangements weren't new, weren't unlawful but they were, for some reason, still a taboo.

On one thing, Vino had been absolutely clear: there'd be no expectation that I'd win before the Tour, and hence no pressure. Travelling to Oman for the first race of my season in February, I was pleasantly nervous, excited by the prospect of a new adventure. I'd also been training well – and hard. My last big session before travelling had been a tough, six-hour effort on Zwift. It's pretty much standard practice to do a final 'hit out' three days before racing, but that's sometimes complicated by a long journey to the race location or jet lag, so you have to be flexible. I'd done Oman before, and the schedule was always the same: an overnight charter that everyone took, straight to the hotel for breakfast and then two easy days of riding to taper down before racing. My 'formula' for the week had worked before so would work again … or so I thought. One of the team's directeurs had other ideas. Alexandr Shefer was a former rider, a former climber, a Kazakh by birth but, by now, after decades racing and working in Italian teams, a committed Italophile in language and also cycling culture. With me, he'd also already been conspicuously standoffish, maybe because he didn't speak a word of English but perhaps also, I sensed, because he didn't have a lot of time for sprinters.

Now, having just got off the plane and arrived at the hotel, we sat at the breakfast table – a group of me, Shefer and two of our Italian riders, Manuele Boaro and Leonardo Basso. Shefer spoke in Italian. Not realising that I also speak Italian.

'*Facciamo 100 chilometri. Perché lui ieri ha fatto solo rulli.*'

'We're doing 100 kilometres. Because he' – and here he nodded sniffily in my direction – 'only rode on rollers yesterday.'

And with that he got up and walked away. Leaving me to ask the others, 'Did he just say what I think he said? That I "only" rode on the rollers yesterday?'

In actual fact 'only' doing six hours on the rollers was equivalent to doing eight on the road, as anyone who knows anything about cycling is aware. But that was by the by. The bigger worry was that one of the prominent decision-makers in our team patently regarded me with a diffidence bordering on contempt that I could practically smell on his breath. I'd been here before, with Wilfried Peeters at QuickStep. He eventually softened to the extent that, years after our fractious introduction, when I won at the Tour in 2021, his tears of joy nearly flooded northern France. But I couldn't or didn't want to take the risk again. My soigneur finally convinced Shefer, in Russian, that I knew my body and what it needed before the first race of the season. But it would be months – not until the Giro d'Italia – before I finally started to break through Shefer's permafrost exterior.

As during my hunt for a team the previous autumn and on so many other occasions during my career, I was plunged into introspection: why did I find it so hard to win people's confidence? Or why were there certain character types, or people in certain roles, that seemed impervious to whatever success I had, whatever charm offensive I employed – or, conversely, whatever authentic face I tried to present? By now, I wasn't narcissistic enough to expect or demand universal popularity, and I knew I had my flaws. If it was my personality, I could understand it. But I was still flummoxed when I encountered a hostility that obeyed no logic, or seemed grounded in ill-informed prejudice. Once again: there were riders who had built a career on 'potential', bouncing from one huge contract to the next, never really delivering but seemingly never being questioned, yet here I was, 160 wins deep, getting side-eye from a directeur sportif who didn't know me ... but who had already assumed I didn't know how to train.

It had been the mood music in the cycling media for as long as I could remember. And the refrain would be no different throughout the spring of 2023. With one difference, compared to other years and other teams I'd been in: Astana didn't seem to give a flying you-know-what about what the media said. That's maybe going a little too far, or sounds facetious, but the team press officer, a tall, lugubrious 40-something Moldovan called Vitalii Abramov had spelled it out at the training camp in Alicante. There, we'd talked about my media commitments, and I'd said there was one thing he should bear in mind: for whatever reason, drama seemed to follow me around, whether of my own making or the media's invention, and any hint of a controversy would be blown out of proportion. I'd thought I was imparting valuable information but Vitalii just shrugged. 'We don't give a shit,' he said. Which, frankly, was a breath of fresh air.

The team could afford to think differently about public relations because they weren't exactly funded like your average WorldTour team. The main sponsor was a sovereign wealth fund based in the city of Astana, the capital of Kazakhstan since 1997, having replaced Almaty. Other sponsors used cycling teams and the real estate on their jerseys to advertise products or boost brand awareness. Think Lidl supermarkets or Movistar mobile phone plans. Our sponsor–team relationship was more about 'nation building'. Showcasing Kazakhstan as a modern, competitive and internationally engaged country. And not the home of 'Borat'.

With no pressure from the team to give every reporter or photographer their pound of flesh, I barely spoke to the media ... and thereby created a vacuum into which any narrative could be poured. One focused on Max Richeze, who'd been lined up as my lead-out rider at B&B. When that all fell apart, he hadn't found a team and, with his fortieth birthday approaching, had had to retire. Why hadn't Cavendish got him a gig with Astana, Richeze was asked at his farewell race, the Tour of San Juan, which he was racing with his national team? He didn't know, he said, 'but Cavendish stopped answering his phone'.

The websites had their quote but of course the reality was a bit more complex. For starters, the subtext seemed to be that Richeze and I were great friends and that I'd somehow betrayed him – which wasn't really true. We got on well and I rated him as a rider, but we'd never been teammates or friends off the bike. I'd wanted him at B&B partly because he'd be a great tutor and mentor for Cees Bol: I'd watched Max ride in inexperienced lead-out trains before and, unlike other seasoned pros in the same circumstances, patiently guide understudies through the first few months of what were inevitably trial and error. I'd thought he could do the same at B&B. But I'd made no firm commitment to tether his future to mine. When I tried to lobby for him with Vinokourov, Vino wasn't keen, and I told Max that in a call a few days before Christmas. He then texted me on Boxing Day – '*Come va?*' – two words, 'How's it going?' and, admittedly, I wasn't looking at my phone much over Christmas and so there was no reply. Then on 23 January I read that I'd stopped answering the phone and left him hanging. The bottom line, and what I told him in a long message that day, was that I was sorry he wasn't being given the opportunity to finish a long career on his own terms. I also regretted not calling him earlier in January to spell out that Astana still didn't want him but that I'd keep trying. I should have communicated better, so mea culpa. But I didn't believe I'd betrayed him in the way the media was now suggesting.

Soon, predictably, as March flowed into April and April into May, my inability to register a first win in Astana colours became another one of the media narratives of the spring. One article would talk about a 'nadir' being reached in the first week of the Giro d'Italia. 'Just what is going wrong?' the same piece asked.

The reality was that I'd been quietly going about my business. After Oman, I'd had a low-key UAE Tour and a mediocre Tirreno–Adriatico, not sprinting once. Traditionally Tirreno is the last tune-up before Milan–Sanremo, the first 'monument' of the season, which I won at my first attempt in 2009. Now, in the same race 14 years later, there were moments in my seven hours on the bike when I wondered whether my age was finally catching up with me. Or if the pro peloton had accelerated even beyond what I'd observed over the previous few seasons – and beyond my capacities. 'The easiest race to finish and the hardest to win', is the age-old, clichéd characterisation of Sanremo. I duly crossed the line in 150th place, over ten minutes behind the winner, Mathieu van der Poel, and feeling as though I belonged in a different universe. In 2009 I'd hung on over the final, key climb, the Poggio, and then produced what a lot of people still considered the best sprint of my career on the Sanremo seafront. In 2025 I watched the race play out on the Poggio … several hours later, on the TV highlights. Seeing van der Poel sprinting *over the top of the Poggio* was a sobering spectacle.

Days like that dented my confidence but not the faith that the work would eventually pay off. There had been enough encouraging signs. On stage one at the UAE Tour, for example, wind had shredded the bunch from the gun and Cees and I made the front split. I could only get third in the sprint but the day had boosted my morale. I certainly ended that afternoon in better physical and mental shape than one of our Spanish climbers, Javier Romo. He was one of the latest off a lengthening production line of riders with next to no top-level cycling experience who had got themselves noticed with prodigious performances on indoor training applications like Zwift. Poor Javier – who's a lovely guy, incidentally – had never ridden in or maybe even seen an echelon before. He got back to the bus after that stage with his pupils the size of small planets, cheeks like caverns, looking like a shell-shocked soldier.

On reflection, that day in the Arabian desert represented, if not a turning point, then a vivid screenshot of a sense of conflict that now inhabited me. On the one hand I still felt competitive, energised, connected to my team-mates, whereas on the other, somewhere in me, was a growing sense of alienation. From a sport and style of racing that obeyed logic and dogmas that I no longer understood, for one. Teams trying to split a race in the wind when there was no wind, as they had that day; riders parachuted into WorldTour teams because they could generate more power than a hadron collider in the lab but had zero race craft, and might as well have been sitting on a rowing machine as the saddle of a bike.

. . .

Generally I could see, and had done for a while, that this sport was evolving away from me. Some change was undoubtedly progress but, broadly, it was a world that no longer felt like my own. Just like in society in general, all around me I saw more individualism, less collectivism. Too much emphasis on the empirical and not enough on the emotional. If you reduce riders to commodities or the common denominator or whatever performance metric is in vogue that month or that year, what you get is a recipe for disconnection. It was no wonder blokes were running each other off the road, riding as though the only code of conduct that applied was 'kill or be killed'. At the start of my career, cycling was emerging from a time when doping had been its defining existential drama. Now, in the twilight of my life as a pro, it felt like this – a depersonalisation of what used to be a 'society on wheels', to use one of the best definitions of the peloton.

I knew that, even in my inner monologue, I sounded like every old pro – blinkered by nostalgia, poisoned by bitterness. But it was far from outright rejection – which was where the conflict arose. There were elements of the job that I still adored. For example: the challenge of building a group, creating a team, as much as that had become a much harder task in recent years. In the team bus on the way to races, every rider's head was buried in his phone. There was little dialogue and even less laughter. Not much of that nervous energy that I remembered from years earlier – a cocktail of anxiety, anticipation and camaraderie spilling over, filling the aisles of the team bus or the corridors of the hotel. That could still exist, but it would have to be manufactured. I had always recognised the importance of my team in my successes, both publicly and privately, while also knowing – but leaving it to others to point out – that I'd put enormous effort into creating that chemistry. At Astana it was even harder and, therefore, more important, in a team where I'd landed at the last minute, whose racing style had until then been founded on opportunism and individual brilliance, and whose rum amalgam of cultures and language made them the unlikeliest patchwork family. It had been clear to me on that first night in Spain that this would be my biggest challenge. I'd set about it immediately, bringing a deck of cards to every race, getting everyone involved every night after dinner. Fighting the temptation to do what I knew almost every other rider in every other team was doing – finishing their dinner and going straight back to their room to scroll through social media or call their families. I felt the same urge but I also had a family that I was trying to build here. Every day, from dawn until dusk, I had to invest in that too. And, sure enough, the more I put in, the more we all got out: more fun, more laughs, more mutual understanding and more strength to draw on later in the year, when it most mattered.

This could all seem like a means to an end – the ultimate goal and the ultimate joy for any rider of winning – but in my case it was also an end in itself. I was by now under no illusion that, as much as I protested or rejected the notion, my career would be at least partly defined by whether or not I finally won a thirty-fifth Tour de France stage. The public and the press could use this as their yardstick … but that didn't prevent me from finding pride and gratification elsewhere. Watching team-mates develop and thrive, for example. Or simply find themselves, in a sport that was increasingly fetishising but also eating its young. Depersonalising and commodifying them. Failing to listen to and understand them.

This could be another one of my goals. A passion project far more important than a number – some statistical quirk brought up in every interview. Something that would really change lives.

I'd finish the spring of 2023 with no actual victories on the road but a small, maybe important one in this particular arena.

CHAPTER 6

n a sport whose allure had once resided in its exoticism but was slowly being demystified, homogenised and – especially – anglicised, there remained one or two final frontiers to the understanding of even someone like me, who had seen and experienced pretty much the lot.

Globalisation had come in a few stages to professional cycling. For most of its history, the sport existed, almost hermitically sealed within the perimeters of western Europe. Every once in a while, some maverick pioneer from, say, Australia or Canada would clamber over the figurative wire fence and make history as that nation's first representative in the Tour de France or some other race. But the trickles almost never became a flood. Sometimes it took seismic geopolitical shifts to bring about meaningful change – for example, the fall of the Berlin Wall in 1989, which finally cleared the way for athletes from former communist states. Or the success of a couple of trailblazers suddenly opening eyes and pathways for a whole continent, as occurred with the Colombians and South America, also in the 1980s. That same decade, the first Tour de France victory by an

American, Greg LeMond, would eventually be regarded as a catalytic moment – the spark for true globalisation. Or, if not that, then at least as a dividing line between a parochial past and a truly global future.

There were still unexplored and certainly grossly under-represented territories, like the whole continent of Africa. But for the most part it was a sport that, as it became more international, had also started to feel less diverse. Everyone spoke English and inhabited broadly the same cultural common ground. There were few mysteries. Not many enigmas. Nothing and no one that wasn't a few clicks from being easily talent-scouted, decoded or explained.

But, again, there *were* a couple of exceptions. If a Kazakh-registered team was already an oddity, the seemingly revolving cast of ex-Soviet Bloc riders who, every year, accounted for half of Astana's roster – for the most part without ever winning a race or even giving an interview to the international media – remained a source of total bewilderment. They didn't speak English, French or any of the peloton's other common vernaculars; no one knew where *exactly* they'd come from or where they often disappeared to after two or three largely invisible seasons in the team. They were cycling's mythical beasts – our yetis or Loch Ness monsters. They were fascinating – and yet not fascinating enough for anyone to find out more, even in their own team.

In 2023, Gleb Syritsa was one such rider. And I was about to uncover the man behind the mask.

Gleb's passport or Google would tell you that he was born in St Petersburg in April 2000. Since Russia's invasion of Ukraine in 2022, Russia had no longer been recognised by international sporting federations, meaning athletes like Gleb competed with no flag next to their name in official results. The 2022 season was also when Gleb had joined Astana. He was 190 centimetres tall and weighed 85 kilograms – a hulking figure, by professional cycling standards, with the chiselled jaw of a prize fighter, the eyes of a puppy dog and the thighs of a comic-book hero.

I first got to know him at Tirreno–Adriatico in March. I say 'got to know him', but there was little conversation: he could clearly understand some English, the odd word, but wouldn't say anything back. On the bike he was a wrecking ball – all power and no real understanding of where or how to use it. On the hardest day of that race, the sprinters and bigger riders all congregated in the 'gruppetto' – the last group on the road in which everyone works together and towards the common goal of simply finishing inside the time limit. The purpose and etiquette of the gruppetto is so well established that it needs no explanation, certainly not to a professional rider. And yet Gleb either hadn't got the memo or someone, at some point, had given him different rules. At one point on the stage, out of nowhere, he bolted out of the gruppetto like he was sprinting for the finish line. I couldn't believe what I was seeing. He soon boomeranged back to us, then a few minutes later was doing the same thing again:

rising out of the saddle, hammering the pedals and disappearing down the road. Then, a few more minutes later, getting caught and passed by us again. It was one of the most bizarre pieces of riding I'd ever seen.

After the second or third time, I rode alongside and almost literally collared him. 'Gleb! Gleb?! What the fuck are you doing? CHILL OUT! Do you see all these guys in this group? We've been doing this for years. Just watch us and stay in the wheels! Fuck's sake.'

He half-nodded but emitted a sound – a mumble – that suggested he didn't agree. So I told him again, 'Just fucking chill out!'

I'd never seen a guy with so much nervous energy. He was clearly an impressive physical specimen, but he was missing education on how to ride. Or, more importantly, how to relax. In the hotel, in the evenings, he ate like he raced – tearing through plate after plate, until you thought he was going to burst and the contents of his stomach pebbledash the walls. Occasionally one of us would crack a joke, or smile in his direction, and he'd giggle back, but that was as far as the communication went.

After Tirreno, there was a week before Sanremo, broken up by Milano–Torino on the Wednesday. Teams would traditionally base themselves somewhere near Milan for the whole week. It was mainly a week to take a breath, recover for the two races, Milano–Torino and then the big one, Sanremo. Hence, on the first night, when arrived at what would be our 'home' for the week, I laid down the law: tonight, I told Gleb, he was coming with me and Cees Bol for a burger and a beer. No questions, no buts – that was what we were doing. He needed to learn to relax, I told him, and he could start here and now by doing as I said.

We weren't going to turn him into the Big Lebowski overnight, but it was a start. And, as it turned out, a case of one step forward, two steps back: the next day, when Cees came down for our 'recovery ride' at 11am, we asked the team mechanic if by any chance he'd seen Gleb. Yes, came the answer … about four hours earlier. Gleb had left for training at 7am in the morning.

It was both fascinating and exasperating. Why was no one helping this kid? Giving him some guidance? At this point *he* couldn't give me much insight, so I started asking around. It appeared there was someone steering him, mentoring him, but that person was a couple of thousand kilometres away in the far north of Russia. Gleb never used his actual name, referring only to 'The Chef' or 'The Boss'. It was The Chef who was apparently telling him to train for seven hours the day before a race, The Chef who told him what to eat. The Chef who told him how many hours to sleep.

It would be a while before I found out much more about this Chef, what his real name was and what his credentials were. For now I just observed Gleb in wonder and bamboozlement. At Milano–Torino our lead-out train

ended up derailing at a series of roundabouts in the closing kilometres. This meant a lengthy and animated debrief
about the lack of real-time 'route guidance' from our direc-
tors – basically them telling us over the radio which side
of the roundabout we should take – plus a mea culpa from
me for not having done my homework. Everyone had had
their say ... except Gleb. One of the Russian-speaking
riders then turned to him, more in the spirit of inclusive-
ness than expectation, and we waited. After a second or two
of embarrassed silence, he started speaking ... and, to our
amazement, didn't stop for five minutes. Then came the
'translation' from the team-mate: 'Gleb agrees with everything you all said.'

If that left us none the wiser then he didn't seem to have
learned much in those first few days, either. He finished
Sanremo, barely, having nailed himself to the floor with
seven-hour rides in a week when he should mainly have
been recovering. Those six-and-a-half hours in the saddle at
Sanremo, the longest one-day race in pro cycling, always felt
endless. Evidently, to all except Glebby: before every race
he'd done an extra hour on the rollers before he even got to
the start line.

Gleb wasn't in our team for the Giro di Sicilia, but by
now I was fascinated by the guy. After the race, on the
way to the airport, I began quizzing one of our Russian
doctors, who responded with the weary tone of someone who couldn't fathom the reason for such curiosity.

It turned out that The Chef was the legendary coach in Russian cycling history, Alexander Kuznetsov. This was a name I'd heard before, though I didn't quite know where or when; I was certainly familiar with some of the alumni off Kuznetsov's St Petersburg production line – Ekimov, Berzin, Ignatiev, all 'breakout' stars in the pro peloton at some point over the previous 30-odd years. I'd also heard bits and bobs over the years about the Soviet system, the way promising child athletes were cherry-picked and then put into residential academies or boarding schools with punishing regimens of round-the-clock training. I've since also learned that, among generations of Soviet cycling drill sergeants, The Chef was maybe the most iron-fisted but also the most successful of them all. There were stories of his riders regularly training four times a day, beginning with the pre-breakfast rides that were Gleb's staple. Sometimes, one story went, during layovers, tourists would watch in astonishment as the little man in a tracksuit had his riders thrashing away on rollers, dripping with sweat, in the middle of an airport lounge.

Maybe the most amazing thing about The Chef was that he was still going, apparently as enthusiastic and fearsome as ever, deep into his seventies. A few decades earlier he'd acquired an old chicken farm somewhere between Tarragona and Valencia in Spain and that had become his new 'overseas headquarters', where several generations of riders had got their first taste of southern European conditions. The old chicken farm was also where Gleb still lived. The Chef didn't have the same political or financial backing he could rely on under the Soviet regime, but, fortunately, another revenue stream had since presented itself: in the first two decades of the 2000s, his daughter, Svetlana Kuznetsova, had become one of the best and richest tennis players in the world, a double Grand Slam winner. It was with her money that The Chef had apparently built a new velodrome in St Petersburg.

My gentle enquiries to the doctor had now turned into something more akin to a cross-examination. I asked him why no one was helping Gleb, why he was being left to drift. The doctor shrugged. 'It's no good.' He sighed. 'He won't listen ...'

In my head an idea had started to germinate. I paused for a second. Did I really want to say this? *Fuck it*, I thought, and then spoke.

'What if you just give him to me for a couple of weeks? I'll look after him. I've got nearly two weeks in Mallorca now to get ready for the Giro. I'll be with my family – I've hired a villa, we've got a spare room ...'

Silence. Except for the cogs in the doc's head I could hear turning. He hadn't seen this coming ...

'Seriously,' I said. 'He needs some help. Let's just try. I mean, what harm can it do?'

Finally the doc said it wasn't up to him – we'd have to talk to Vino and the management. And, of course, The Chef would have to give his blessing. We were literally having this conversation on the way to the airport, a few hours before I was due on a direct flight to Mallorca. It was, shall we say, a bit spur of the moment. But, after a flurry of phone calls, before I boarded the plane, we had the green light. Gleb would be waiting for me at the other side, in arrivals at Palma airport.

Naturally I'd checked with Peta, but I knew it wouldn't be an issue. I'd grown up as a bike rider relying on the hospitality of former or current riders in locations all over the world. It was simply part of the cycling heritage that I'd absorbed, a sort of unspoken tradition or code for the furtherance of the species, if you will. I'd never forgotten how much I learned in my first few months as a pro living with Roger Hammond, and I'd tried to do the same for younger riders ever since. We'd had Tao Geoghegan Hart staying with us years before he won the Giro d'Italia, and various others who had also, I'd like to think, benefitted just from a few weeks of observing me, training with me, picking my brains. They'd seen how fundamental Peta and family were to my success. She'd also embraced it – that is our 'role' as hosts, guides, friends – whatever it turned out to be. It would be no different now with Gleb.

And so I walked through the sliding doors, into arrivals, and there he was, big smile on his face, a bike bag in each hand – one for the track and one for the road. We then picked up a hire car and headed for the villa. Peta and the kids were arriving later in the day, so in the meantime, we unpacked our bikes and got them ready. Every surface of Gleb's equipment – every screw, every cable – glistened. He touched and even looked at his bike with the care and pride of a parent with their newborn baby. It made a refreshing change from the dirt-encrusted derailleurs and zero-fucks-given attitudes of a lot of riders from his generation.

In those first hours we communicated as we had at races in those first few months of 2023: with me speaking slowly and in three or maximum four-word, simple sentences, and Gleb nodding or smiling back. Added to the difficulty of expressing himself in English, he had a stammer which became severe when he was stressed, which, it looked to me, was all the time.

I'd pointed him to his room, after which he'd sat on the bed, unsure of what to do. When I appeared in the door-way an hour or so later, he got up from exactly where I'd left him and urgently made his way towards me. He looked even more anxious than usual. As though something terrible had happened.

'Programme? Programme for week?'

Up to this point I'd told him nothing. Deliberately. He needed to chill – to use what was going to be the word of the week – starting from now.

'Gleb,' I said. 'No programme. No programme, no stress. Every morning I'll tell you what we're doing that day. Or, if we're going to the track, I'll tell you the night before. But no stress. Chill. No problem.'

I might as well have been telling a shark not to swim. He looked even more terrified now.

That night we took him for dinner. Me, the whole family and Gleb. I'd wanted to do it ever since, earlier in the year, Cees Bol had sent me a picture of him and Gleb at an airport, on the way home from a race, Gleb with a big hamburger in his hand. Cees had taken and sent the photo because Gleb had never been to a proper restaurant before. This was apparently as close as he'd come.

I know a chef who was a big cycling fan and owned a restaurant on the other side of Palma, so I'd called him and booked us in. Beautiful place. Quite fancy. We arrived, sat down and I saw Gleb's eyes and smile widen as a waiter arrived with the menus. His expression wouldn't change for the next two hours, as I ordered champagne, oysters, foie gras – the lot – to make sure his first restaurant meal was going to be one to remember. A few times, there'd be something left on one of the plates, and either Peta or I would offer it around the table, being polite, as you do. Well, whatever it was, however much else he'd eaten, Gleb would just gleefully add it to the food already piled on his plate.

'Living his best life' didn't begin to cover it. Honestly, it was one of the most enjoyable dinners of my life – not because of what we ate, as delicious as it was, but just because I'd rarely seen such joy.

When we got back that night, maybe loosened up by a couple of glasses of wine, Gleb also started to open up.

Finally we were able to fill in a few more pieces to the puzzle: his relationship with his mum, who he called every day, and who had been one of Russia's leading free divers; his dad, who had also been an athlete; and, maybe most significant, the day when, at age 11, he was hanging out with friends in a skatepark and felt a hand on his shoulder. He turned around to see a man who proceeded to tell him that that he had been selected for training as a … cyclist. He'd soon be enrolled in a specialist school, presided over by the great Kuznetsov, the man told him. From the moment he was formally enrolled shortly thereafter until the present day – April 2023 in Mallorca – Gleb reckoned he'd spent about four days in his family home.

The more Gleb talked, the more what I'd seen in those first few races of the year made sense. He told me that, eventually, The Chef had deemed him ready for the next step in his development and moved him to the old chicken farm in Spain. There they would train much as they had in St Petersburg, starting with the sacrosanct one hour on rollers before breakfast, and continuing for four hours on the road, when they weren't allowed to talk and certainly couldn't stop for a coffee or a piece of cake, until lunchtime. In the afternoon, they'd do two relatively easy hours, but, again, with no interaction – and sometimes even all riding at the same pace, scattered across the road at 500 metre intervals. Dinner was either salmon and rice or chicken and pasta. Although the days hardly varied, they'd receive their training plan six weeks in advance and be expected to complete every session, come rain or shine, even if they were ill. The Chef had used the same formula, supposedly with great success, for 40 years, so if it wasn't broke …

I put it to Gleb that, in actual fact, given that perhaps 10,000 or more kids had been through The Chef's system over several decades, and only a handful had made the grade as pro riders, maybe his wasn't such a recipe for success after all. But, to this, Gleb would just shrug. Even if he was inclined to consider alternatives, he was simply too institutionalised; The Chef had given him a home in Spain, residency, and all of the collateral benefits that came with that, like visa-free travel at a time when his homeland was at war and increasingly isolated. Defying The Chef meant losing everything, Gleb wanted me to understand. He would be like Russia – cut off, cut adrift. He'd had a good friend from Ukraine whom he'd 'lost' after Russia invaded. Gleb also hoped I knew that he just wanted peace … and to be able to race his bike. This was very important.

He would discover the following day that the Cavendish Method was quite different from what he was used to under The Chef, very much by design. On the menu was a brisk, long ride through the hilly western side of Mallorca. After about four hours and numerous attempts on my part to break the ice, Gleb had hardly said a word. We then arrived in the small town of Calvià, which – I immediately noticed – was busier than I remembered. We soon found out why when we swung into town and saw stalls set up all down the main street for the weekly market. It was a fair detour to avoid the chaos ... so I got off my bike and prepared to wheel it to the other end of the street, where we could jump back on. I was doing just that, literally dismounting, when I looked across at Gleb, who was frozen on the spot, still on his bike, his feet still clipped into the pedals. He looked petrified.

When I asked what was wrong, he replied that he couldn't get off his bike. We still hadn't finished our ride, so he couldn't stop pedalling.

At first I thought he was taking the piss. 'You can't ... *what?!*' He wasn't joking. So I asked him what he usually did when he got to traffic lights – ride through? Because he had to stop then, too. He said that was exactly what he did. Because if he stopped, and The Chef saw it on his power files ...

Eventually, here, he had no choice. He didn't know the way home, so would have to wait for me. And I intended to take him out of his comfort zone, or force him to expand it – which I did by taking my time. I noticed a stall selling toys, including firecrackers, which I knew the kids would love. But instead of just quickly picking up a packet, paying and getting on our way, I began a lengthier-than-necessary nego-tiation with the stallholder. It didn't work in the sense that the price remained unchanged: €3(!). But it had the desired effect of forcing Gleb to realise – or at least entertain the idea – that five minutes off our bikes, in a five-hour session, changed absolutely nothing.

We got back to the villa an hour or so later and the afternoon was a riot. The kids loved the firecrackers … and they loved Gleb. My youngest son, Casper, was obsessed with his new mate – this big, friendly giant who'd throw him in the pool – and would gurgle back when Casper made him laugh. 'You see,' I told him. 'We were off our bikes for five minutes and it's given us and the kids, what, two hours of fun?' Gleb grinned back, nervously. There was still, clearly, work to do.

As the days passed, I felt more and more ready for the Giro and, relatively speaking, Gleb also loosened up. After the shopping trip in Calvià, at the end of the next day's ride I made him stop at the bakery in Deià owned by my former team-mate Vicente Reynés. I bought us custard pastries and made Gleb eat his on a terrace overlooking the Mediterranean. 'Look at that,' I told him. 'Isn't it beautiful? Worth stopping for? Yes, you see We've done our training, now we can relax. Chill! No stress!'

It was a case of 'small wins'. I had a three-week Giro d'Italia to prepare for, but, for his benefit, I tried to make the training 'fun'. Or at least a little more varied, a little more creative than the endlessly repetitive sessions he'd been doing for over a decade. We'd sprint for road signs or imagine and try to recreate race situations. I even accomplished what I'd thought was the impossible – on our recovery day, I said he could either do his one-hour early-morning roller session or come with me, not both. He chose the latter. I then suggested we remove our bike computers and put them in our pockets.

Enjoy the freedom of riding for riding's sake. Relax. No stress. Gleb was happy. At the end of the ride, we stopped at a fancy brunch place in Palma and ordered protein pancakes. It was the first time he'd skipped his 'Chef's breakfast' for over a decade. I knew we were getting somewhere when, the next day, Gleb asked whether he could train on his own. A few hours later he sent me a selfie from the same café – him with his big smile, lips caked in cappuccino froth, and his stack of pancakes. Or, even more so, the day when, after training, I announced that, for the kids, we were going to a pirate-themed novelty restaurant on the other side of Palma. When he started to make excuses, say that he'd rather stay at the villa, I cut him short: 'Gleb, mate, you're fucking coming.' Three hours later, he had a bandanna wrapped around his head, a patch over his eye, and was 'Ooh ahhhing' like Jack Sparrow on laughing gas.

The whole experience, just watching him come out of himself over a few days, was life-affirming. By the end of the first week his stammer had almost gone. But it was sad, as well as endearing. He told me about his passion for Hot Wheels toy cars, and as his eyes lit up, I found myself wondering whether he'd had his childhood ripped away in return for his shot at becoming a professional athlete. He said Peta reminded him of his mum … so much so that he started calling her 'Mama'. He told us The Chef didn't believe in riders having families and being able to perform. I tried to explain that it was my secret weapon, that their love and support enhanced my performance rather than impaired it. To this, he nodded thoughtfully.

Before our ways parted on the final day, we went for a last meal, a pizza, just Gleb and me. He was immensely grateful for everything he'd experienced over the previous ten days, but, also, I sensed, still a little confused about my motives. A few days earlier he'd asked me why I was doing it all – why I'd asked the team if he could come to Mallorca? What was I getting out of it? At the time, it was hard to give him a cogent answer, but, on reflection, I think it was simple: helping him made me and Peta feel good, because we could see it was making him feel good. Opening his eyes. Beyond the tunnel vision with which he was struggling to negotiate his life and career.

This story would be vastly improved if, after Mallorca, Gleb had emerged, transformed, into a utopian future of race victories, personal fulfilment and spiritual enlightenment. Alas, that's not quite how it turned out, although over the next few months, with some satisfaction and pride, I did see Gleb change and even start to finally, shall we say, emancipate himself. Already well liked, he became maybe the most universally beloved rider in the team – 190 centimetres and 85 kilograms of muscles, heart and, yes, brain. In the evenings, at races, if he wasn't in his room reading Tolstoy or Dostoevsky, he'd be orchestrating card games with the deck that now went with him everywhere. Soon, he'd have a girlfriend. He also hadn't forgotten our ten days in Mallorca – and sent Peta or 'Mama' a set of Russian dolls as a thank you.

On the road, though, old habits seemed to die harder. He was now questioning if not outright defying The Chef, and, for the first time, The Chef was making concessions. But change was going to be a slow process. Gleb would win two stages of the Tour de Langkawi later in the year, but in the more prestigious races, with high-quality fields, he would sometimes get close, but no cigar. He needed the kind of day-to-day, up-close nurturing I'd given him in Spain, and in a team of 30 riders and 70 staff that was never going to happen. The management either lost faith in his potential quickly or didn't have much in the first place. In desperate need of ranking points to stave off relegation to cycling's 'second division', at the end of 2024, they'd decide his place in the team would be better filled by someone else, and relegated him to Astana's development or feeder team.

For me, that was a disappointing outcome to what had been an instructive and rewarding but also, in a way, quite sad experience. The previous 20 years had taught me plenty about opportunity, nature versus nurture, and the short-termism that prevailed in this sport. They had also demonstrated to me, emphatically, that if I had a gift and a passion, one greater than sprinting for finish lines, it was extracting the best out of other bike riders. I was not Freud, I had no degree in psychology, but I could unlock potential on a bike, not only my own but also that of the riders around me. With Gleb I had played the part of teacher, but he had given me this lesson or reminder – and maybe a glimpse of a future fast approaching.

That would all come soon enough. First I was on my way to the Giro d'Italia.

CHAPTER 7

After the crash in Gent, 2021. I'd been rushed to intensive care and all the painkillers had me feeling like I was flying.

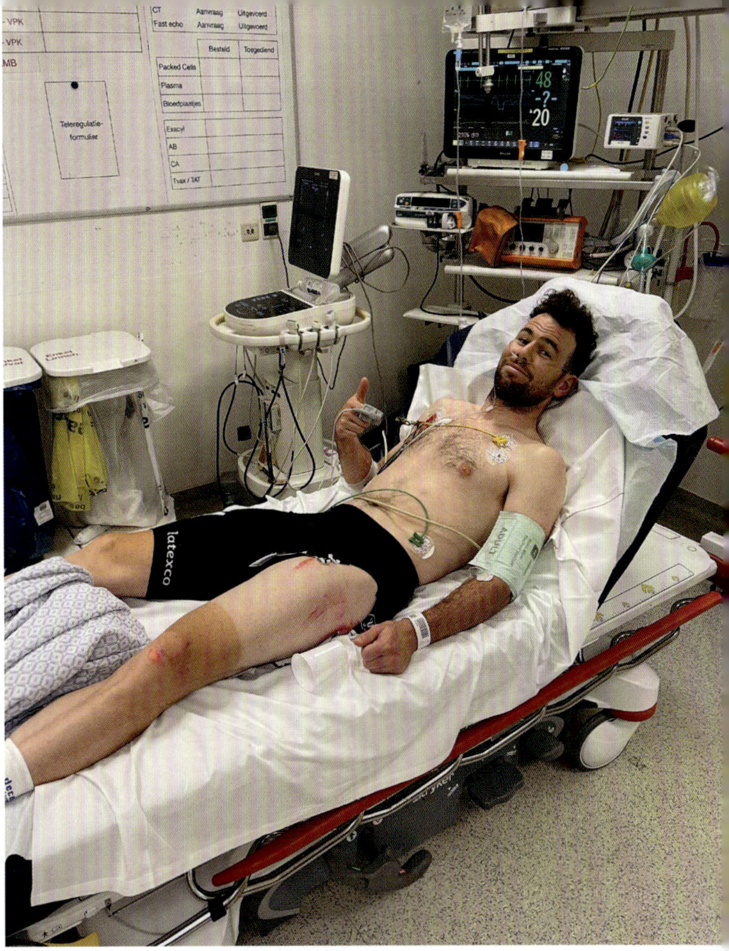

Winning the British Nationals in 2022 after a crazy ride in Cumbria. I'd proven myself but I still wouldn't be selected for the Tour that year.

A hard January training session with QuickStep.

Taking Casper, my mini-me, training.

A family visit to the Giro in 2023, where I'd announce my retirement.

Gianni and Joe by my side. My soldiers at the Giro in 2023.

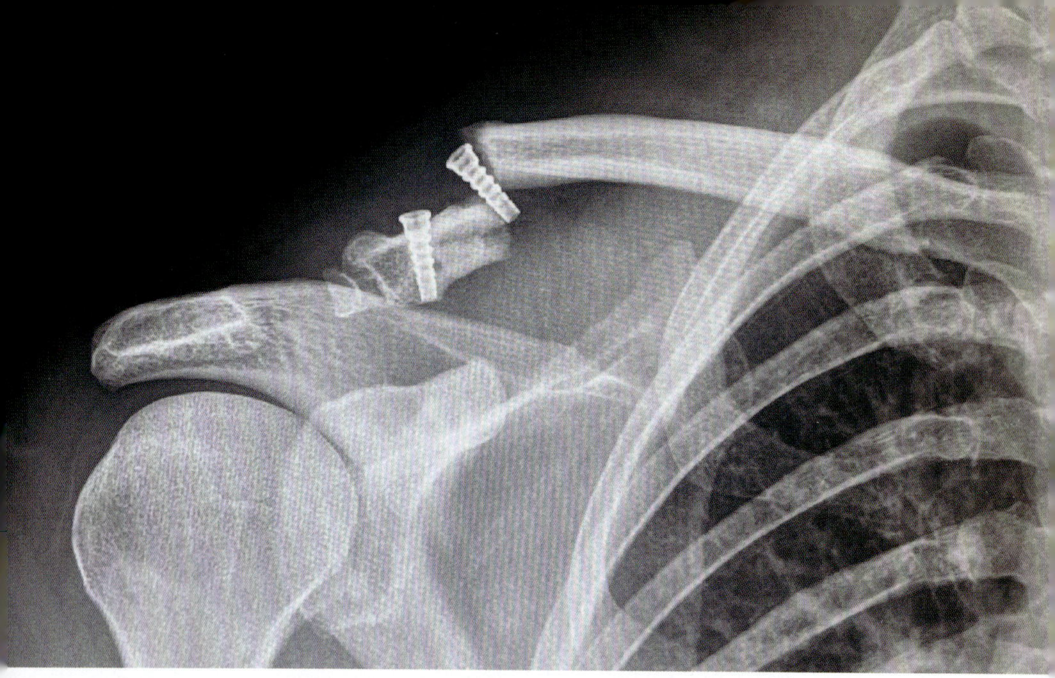

An X-ray of my broken collarbone after the 2023 crash.
I wasn't sure if that would be how my final Tour ended.

After years of not speaking, Sagan and I made up.
This was taken in Tokyo.

Out in Mallorca with Gleb and the family, where I introduced him to the Cavendish Method.

Quite different to what he was used to …

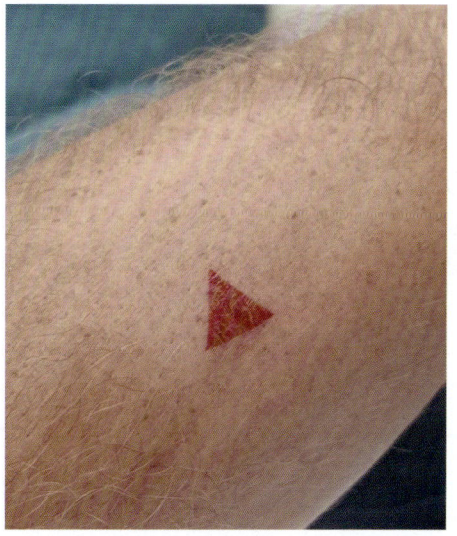

My 'Flamme Rouge' tattoo, signifying the start of the final kilometre in a bike race and what defined me in my sport. The final push.

Riding with Vino – a manager with a rider's heart.

Training after descending from 2,300 metres above sea level in the Sierra Nevada mountains.

Emptying the tank in Greece during our last ten days of prep.

Vasi rode with me on recovery days.

My surrogate Greek family. It was Vasi's son who came up with my alter-ego.

My 35th stage win. Astrid was the only one of my children who hadn't yet stood with me on a Tour de France podium. I'm glad we could rectify that.

With the boys – Ballerini, Bol and Tejada – finishing my last ever mountain as a pro bike rider.

At what point in a man's life does he begin to feel officially 'old'? And what is the precise physiological or psychological trigger?

No doubt some people would answer that, in their experience, it was reaching a certain age or milestone – say a fortieth birthday or the arrival of a first child. Or, no doubt, for some, there was no clearly delineated *Eureka!* or *Oh Fuck!* moment – only a random day, in a miscellaneous week, when they looked in the mirror and saw a face like the road maps I've studied for 20-odd years before every bike race, only with each line representing a journey already navigated, rather than one they still had to make.

Most, I'm guessing, would describe a sad but materially meaningless realisation – but for athletes it's different. For us, if such a moment existed, it would carry the double jeopardy of a message telling us that our life, or one life at least, was nearing its end point. That the cornerstone upon which we'd carefully constructed our livelihood and identity – our exceptional bodies, primarily – had reached a point of decay where we would soon be absorbed into the mediocre masses. The beginning of a death sentence.

Besides the fact that I, too, would celebrate another trip around the sun in the month of May, my thirty-eighth, and that the media seemed as obsessed with my retirement date as they were about the Merckx record, there had been no obvious forewarning in the run-up to the Giro. Maybe I was simply too focused or distracted to entertain any thoughts beyond the task at hand. My final race before the Giro had been a stage race in Switzerland, the Tour de Romandie. The team hadn't wanted me to do it, but over the previous few years my tried and tested formula before Grand Tours had worked as follows: after an extremely hard block of training like what I'd done with Gleb in Mallorca – with intense track sessions designed to cause maximum muscle damage, complemented by long steady road rides – I'd finish off my prep with a short, hilly stage race. I trusted this method and seen it work multiple times … which isn't to say that all the graft immediately bore fruits. On the contrary, in fact, that last, tune-in race had often been a disaster, results-wise, and Romandie would be no different.

The Tour de Romandie was supposed to last six days. Mine didn't even stretch to two: I climbed into a team car midway through the second afternoon and was soon on my way to the airport. The team put out a statement to say that I was ill. Really I was just … fucked, mentally and physically.

The week had started badly when I realised that one of the mechanics had put the wrong wheels on my bike, and for the first time since joining the team I'd lost my rag. The wheels could be swapped and I could, and did, apologise, but these blow-ups left a cloud of embarrassment that tended to linger. More to the point, on that second day INEOS had attacked almost from the gun – yet another one of those moves that were becoming increasingly common in modern cycling, the logic of which totally escaped me. My already dark mood now turned black. Dropped, I impatiently waved away my team-mates' attempts to help me and was soon peeling off my race number.

While the media declared a new low point in what looked to them like an inexorable downward spiral, I wasn't unduly concerned. I had bigger things to worry about than what they said – like for instance how we were going to improvise a lead-out train at the Giro in an eight-man team made up predominantly of climbers with zero experience of setting up a sprinter. Or how I was going to get through three weeks taking orders from Alexandr Shefer – the directeur sportif who in Oman had wanted to send me out for 100 kilometres the day before the race because six hours on an indoor bike wasn't 'proper' training.

It was just as well that the team was not putting any pressure on me to win or, for that matter, finish the race in Rome in three weeks. It was common for sprinters to ride the first two weeks of the Giro and pull out before the biggest mountains so as not to go too deep before the Tour de France. Sprint opportunities were concentrated in that first fortnight – starting, this time, with stage two along the Adriatic coast. To my pleasant surprise, that day, the lads made up for in effort and commitment what they lacked in practice and refinement. We were in good position, nicely lined up, poised to surge … until a crash in front of me with four kilometres to go completely derailed us. Unfortunately, this was to be the story of the next few stages: good legs, good intentions and for the most part good execution, all sabotaged by bad luck and, day after depressing day, unfathomably shitty weather.

A fortnight into the race I think we'd counted a single stage when it hadn't rained. In Salerno halfway through week one I nearly achieved a first in my career: a Grand Tour stage win having finished the race on my arse, aquaplaning across the finish line after another crash in yet another downpour. I came fourth, but the photo went around the world – a metaphor for the current state of Cavendish's career: in a storm, on its backside, dignity gone. Lost in the condescension was that fact that I'd nearly won.

Generally, it was tough going. Wet and cold weather, day after day, in stage races becomes a slow-release poison for the mind and the immune system. You can mummify yourself in wet-weather gear, swig hot tea, grit your teeth so hard they won't chatter, but over several hours, invariably, your body temperature will dip into a danger zone where infections become unavoidable. Suddenly, after a few days of the same misery, half of the peloton is coughing and spluttering, and there's no escape. The bunch becomes a rolling Petri dish, a Mardi Gras of germs, viruses and bacteria.

Inevitably, I'd also get ill, like several of my team-mates. Despite this and another motley pick 'n' mix of characters, nationalities and languages, the mood in the team was generally upbeat, or at least lightened by gallows humour. I roomed with Joe Dombrowski, the bookish but also slightly gauche American who'd helped me 'integrate' at the training camp in January. Joe was hard to dislike … although dislike him, in the first half of the Giro, one rider in our team, Gianni Moscon, certainly did. This wasn't entirely surprising in that, besides both being professional cyclists and Astana, the pair had little or nothing in common. Gianni came from a family of apple farmers in the mountains of northern Italy, had a passion for tractors and a general approach to life that you might also describe as a little 'rustic' or 'agricultural'. He'd started his career with a bang and been touted as the next Italian superstar, but got himself tangled up in various controversies and somehow lost his way.

Since then Gianni had, shall we say, opened his mind, but he could still be a very blunt instrument. In all honesty, I like this about him. You know where you stand. Whether you agree or not. And he expects this to be reciprocated.

If he's done something well, tell him. If he's done something not so well, also tell him. But just be straight. I should also add that my frustration with Joe to a certain extent foregrounded Gianni completely losing his temper later in the race. It had all started on the stage to Naples, the day after my painful crash in Salerno. There, on the last climb of the day up the lower slopes of Mount Vesuvius, I started slipping inexorably backwards through and eventually out of the main peloton. Instinctively, I looked around for help and, within a few seconds of each other, saw Gianni, another Italian, Samuele Battistella, and Joe. Gianni and Samuele immediately slowed to pace me back towards the convoy of team cars and the remnants of the bunch; whether distracted, disinterested or unaware, Joe just rode straight on. Not because he was in contention for a stage win or a high GC position. Just because, well, maybe that was Joe.

I was never going to win that stage, either, but it got worse: as we swung off the descent, down towards the coast, a huge, sudden gust of wind took the bike from under me and dumped me on the tarmac. Again. Understandably, my mood when we got to the hotel that night was decidedly subdued. I had too much fondness for Joe to unload on him, and in fact it was in the spirit of 'kindness' that I gently 'debriefed' him at the end of the day. In short, I said, he might see himself as a bit of a lone wolf in the team, a one-man band who wasn't necessarily relying on his team-mates, but that isolating himself both on and off the bike wouldn't serve the team and wouldn't serve him either. Gianni, for one, had already decided that Joe was not a team player. Now I was essentially telling Joe to prove him wrong, and that what I'd needed on the climb hadn't been for him to completely bury himself or jeopardise his own race. A few seconds of shelter or a word of encouragement would have done, not because it mattered whether I finished in 60th or 120th place, but because it was from moments and situations like this that real spirit was forged. One day that same comradeship would be the difference between victory and defeat.

On the bike, Joe course-corrected immediately, and was exemplary for the rest of the Giro. Unfortunately, off the bike, it took a couple more days to learn the lesson. After one mountain stage, as was often the case because he was the superior climber, Joe finished and got back to the team bus 20-odd minutes before Gianni. Every day, we were given a choice of pasta or rice for a recovery snack that'd be waiting for us. On this day Joe apparently wolfed down his own portion ... then was clearly given the impression by someone, probably one of the soigneurs, that there was a spare box of pasta that he could also take. Cue Gianni arriving, asking for his pasta and being told there was none left because Joe had eaten his.

Important life lesson: never come between an Italian and his pasta. Especially never come between Gianni Moscon and his pasta. After words had been exchanged on the bus, we wondered what version of Gianni would come down to dinner at the hotel that night. That question was answered when he appeared in the doorway of the dining room, took one look at where Joe was sitting and made a beeline for a huge chafing dish full of pasta on the buffet table on the other side of the room. Moments later, he was looming over Joe and slinging an enormous plate of macaroni onto the table in front of him.

'You want more pasta? Even more?! Here you go, take this …'

It was one of those very awkward situations where almost everyone laughs, only to realise that neither the instigator nor the victim of the 'joke' seems particularly amused. Gianni had made his 'point', but that didn't seem to be enough. He kept raising his voice – 'Go on, you wanted pasta! Take it!' – until I had to intervene, forcefully, and tell him to let it go.

It might have turned quite ugly, but Joe, of course, apologised. And then something strange happened: over the next few days Joe and Gianni first started to tolerate each other, then to talk to each other, and eventually – it looked to me – even quite like each other.

It was perhaps just that kind of Giro: if you didn't cry, you could only laugh. I was doing my best to stay upbeat but, stirring in me, somewhere, was a nagging feeling of unease and displacement. I couldn't quite put my finger on it, but at times I felt like I didn't belong – as though I was watching from behind a Perspex screen, rather than participating in the Giro. The suffering was a real as ever, certainly just as painful, but somehow it felt less visceral or existential. As though my legs were stinging but my soul was disengaging, leaving my physical body. Maybe already drifting into some kind of cycling afterlife.

I also couldn't escape another feeling, a different type of alienation: from the other riders in the peloton, my peers. I could no longer relate to them. Or at least not to the way they thought about and approached racing. I saw 'tactics' that broke my brain, attacks and strategies that seemed to follow no logic. They were prevailing trends or mentalities that made me fear for where cycling was going and pine for the sport I'd once known. Maybe I'd become a cycling 'boomer' … but even acknowledging that didn't make some of what I was seeing more comprehensible, or less irritating. If I had to identify a tipping point it was stage ten. That day we were due to climb up through the Apennines, the mountains that bisect the boot of Italy, on roads I've trained on hundreds of times. By now we didn't even need to consult the forecast: we instinctively expected rain, and that was what we got at the start in Scandiano, and what was apparently falling on the hills. To listen to some riders in other teams that morning, though, you'd have thought we were riding into an Arctic blizzard: they wanted the 'Extreme Weather Protocol' invoked, the biggest mountain pass of the day removed from the route and the stage shortened.

I was still sick and wasn't particularly relishing another day in the cold and wet, either. But I couldn't, in good conscience, pretend that these conditions justified the stage being rerouted. Maybe more to the point, I was also tired of what was now an all-too-familiar pantomime, particularly in the Giro. Nowadays it'd start with a flurry of WhatsApp messages between senior riders the night before a stage that, based on someone's weather forecast, at some point, was going to turn nasty. In the space of a few hours, into the next morning, the riders' union would get involved, ask the race organisers for some sort of concession, which would usually be batted away, after which there'd be more conversations, threats, some kicking off on social media and, finally, an outcome that left one or more parties aggrieved. Every year it was the same and, to some extent, such had always been the difficulty of finding a consensus in a sport with so many different and competing interests. On this particular day I was just tired of it – tired of the same old nonsense. I'd even reluctantly gone along with the guys lobbying for a route change, in a desperate and as it turned out naive attempt to achieve some sort of unity. But the 'right' decision was finally taken and the original 'parcours' retained; I was then absolutely flabbergasted when some of the riders who'd lobbied most vociferously for the Extreme Weather Protocol to be applied were among the first riders to attack, senselessly, as soon as the start flag was raised.

Once upon a time, as a younger rider, I would have tried to understand. But now something in me just snapped. I was past anger, maybe past caring. Perhaps my memory was playing tricks, but I'd come from an era in professional cycling when the clearest representation of how collectivism could be balanced with individualism was the way the peloton raced. The watching spectator might have seen us soft-pedalling through the first few hours of every race and felt frustrated by what looked like an unspoken pact of non-aggression. That 'pact' did exist, but underlying it was a sort of pragmatism and emotional intelligence: the knowledge that it was in no one's interest to kick seven bells out of each other every day and for the whole day. Maybe a bit before my time, there'd been a dark side to the peloton's 'honour code', certainly in relation to doping but also, on occasion, intimidation and bullying. On the whole, though, the pro peloton that I'd arrived in as a spiky 21-year-old upstart had felt like a family – perhaps dysfunctional, but a family nonetheless. A community in which, broadly speaking, people looked after each other because they lived and worked together, inhabited the same spaces, shared the same dreams and anxieties. Sometimes, 15 years on, it seemed as though genuine comradeship based on real empathy was a luxury that young riders simply couldn't afford. You could blame mobile phones, the pace of modern life, the anxiety of knowing that their every move in and out of races could be tracked and analysed … Whatever it was, to me they looked like strangers even to each other, among contemporaries, never mind in their relationships towards me. This then translated into a racing style which was spectacular to watch but also indiscriminate, heedless, an exercise in 'kill or be killed'.

These were mainly reflections that crystallised and gained definition later. In the fog of the moment, on that tenth stage, as the rain hammered the tarmac, I made my decision: I'd had enough. I was done with professional cycling.

As I turned the pedals that day and the next, some semblance or outline of a plan began to take shape. I would still, of course, ride the Tour de France in July, but it would be my last one. I was also fed up of the questions, or even just undercurrent of – 'Is this your last season?' – even when that wasn't the question being asked. So I decided not to leave the press or the public waiting any longer: I would make my announcement before the end of the Giro. Before that there were clearly people who needed or deserved to know in advance: family and friends, naturally, but also the team, sponsors, people who'd been part of the journey. Two days before my birthday, the Giro was due to ride into Switzerland over the Great St Bernard Pass, only for bad weather to intervene again and, this time, leave the commissaires and race organisers with no choice but to move the

start a couple of hours' drive closer to the finish. My journey in the team bus was spent making calls and sending text
messages that, clearly, took a few recipients by surprise.

I don't know what, if anything I'd hoped for or expected
from my retirement announcement before that day, but
suddenly, the morning after my thirty-eighth birthday (and
on my youngest son Casper's), there I sat in a hotel conference room just outside Brescia, at the point of no return.
Peta and the kids were at my side. Only a dozen or so journalists were in the room and maybe half that number of
TV crews. Almost for the first time since the start of the
Giro, the sun illuminated a cobalt-blue sky, its rays flooding
in through the window and into my eyes. I gave a short
speech, my voice faltering slightly as I said the words 'This
will be my last season as a professional cyclist.' I thanked my
family, then took a few questions. It was all over quickly. The
journalists then dispersed while I played football with the
kids on the lawn outside the hotel. I could immediately feel
something different: a lightness. The closure that I hadn't
known I needed but obviously did. The clarity I also needed
to focus on that one, last, important but, in my mind, not
career-defining goal: a final win in the Tour de France.

• • •

We had a week still to race in Italy. A lot of sprinters traditionally pulled out at this point – the second rest day – but

one of my peculiarities or strengths as a rider was that I generally improved over the course of a Grand Tour, and had also done better in Tours de France having previously completed the Giro. At the start two weeks earlier, in Abruzzo, I'd also made it my mission to get to Rome and over all the mountains as a point of pride vis-à-vis our directeur sportif, Alexandr Shefer. I'd got the sense right from the start of the year that, in Shefer's mind, only climbers were 'proper' cyclists. Fortunately, over the previous two weeks he'd 'warmed' to me considerably, and me to him. If there was an emotional reason to finish the Giro, it would no longer be about scoring points against him or anyone else: my motivation, my inspiration, over the last week, through soaring Alps and towering Dolomites, would be expressing my gratitude to the Italian fans, the *tifosi*. At no other race, in no other country, was I feted, flattered and in fact hero-worshipped like at the Giro, in Italy. Now, my farewell announcement a few days earlier made the big mountain stages feel like our final communion – me and them in some of cycling's most awe-inspiring, hallowed arenas, the natural cathedrals of the Dolomites, each expressing our mutual love and appreciation.

As always in Grand Tours, over the course of the three weeks, 3,500 kilometres and 50,000 metres of elevation, every rider's world and perspective closed in. I was part of a race, a peloton and a team, but in the last week, in the mountains, with survival mode fully engaged, there was no room for peripheral vision. The battle for the pink jersey and overall victory had been raging for three weeks, increasingly out of my sight – many minutes up the road on some stages – and out of mind. Usually at this point in a three-week race I could barely even tell you who was in second or third place overall, but here I had a vested interest, a dog in the fight: one of my oldest friends in cycling, Geraint Thomas, at 37, had led the race since stage ten. With 'only' a mountain time trial to Monte Lussari on the Slovenian border then the formality of the final sprint stage in Rome to ride, G led Primož Roglič by 26 seconds.

The logistics of the time trial were such that riders would start in two waves, with me in the first chunk, early in the morning, and G the last rider to go late in the afternoon. Before leaving for my start time, I texted him: 'Go fucking smash it today, mate.' If there was anyone I knew who wouldn't be panicking in this situation, who could ride the TT of his life like it was a village kermesse, it was G.

The road up Monte Lussari was a stairway to hell, a tarmac drainpipe. I had nothing to gain but plenty to lose in the sense that, on a stage like this, the time cut posed a real threat. Nonetheless, through gritted teeth and by sticking to a plan – a predetermined number of watts to push all the way up – I made it safely to the top while also savouring the atmosphere. The mountain throbbed with noise – specifically, fans screaming my name. The last couple of kilometres and hideous final ramps made a nice metaphor for my 15 years of riding the Giro: a full-bodied distillation of love, joy and suffering.

By lunchtime, Gianni Moscon and I had been driven to our team hotel near Venice. We'd fly to Rome the next morning and race the last stage in the late afternoon, which gave us well over 24 hours to 'kill'. Our first 'activity': a stroll to the next-door shopping mall – the sole source of any nearby 'entertainment' – and Aperol spritz for two at a café by the entrance to a supermarket, surrounded by punters wheeling their trolleys and schlepping groceries. Then a second spritz. And a third. And fourth. Finally, a bit tipsy, we decided we'd put on a 'watch party' for the end of the TT in one of the soigneurs' rooms, with spritz for everyone. A quick trolly dash and we were soon heading back to the hotel with carrier bags full of grissini, prosciutto, Aprerol, Prosecco and soda water.

As our team-mates started to arrive, it was turning into one of the most fun afternoons I could remember at a Giro – with everyone celebrating our three weeks together, having a drink while watching the race. Unfortunately, it didn't end the way that I – or Geraint – had expected or intended. I watched in disbelief as, having looked comfortably ahead throughout the TT, as the gradient stiffened, G started losing time. Roglič, who had lost the Tour de France in a similar TT three years earlier, looked to have blown his chance again when his chain derailed halfway up the climb. By sheer, unbelievable coincidence, an old mate of his, back from when he was a ski-jumper, was standing at the roadside at that precise point, and helped him get back on and moving again. Turbo-charged by adrenaline, he ended up beating G by 40 seconds to win the stage. Given that for the GC guys the last stage was no more than a procession, it meant that Roglič would win the Giro by the fourth smallest margin in the 114-year history of the race – 14 seconds.

I was utterly heartbroken for Geraint. He'd ridden the perfect race – a masterpiece. I also got on with and liked Roglič, but G was … G. He'd won Olympic titles, the Tour de France, all in the same unpretentious, matter-of-fact way, not courting any hype and, because of that, probably not getting the recognition he deserved. No one had really fancied him for the Giro, either, certainly not at his age, yet he'd quietly, doggedly produced a performance that, when he *should* have stood there in the pink jersey the next day, in the shadow of the Colosseum, *should* have represented a last, glorious monument to his career. Now, it'd be Roglič in pink, and I couldn't begin to imagine how G would feel.

The next morning my head was still spinning, from what we'd seen in TT, not the spritz. I of course still had a job to do in Rome, the Eternal City, where my Giro career would in fact end that night. The last stages of Grand Tours were always a sting in the tale for sprinters when they were set up like this one, destined for a bunch gallop. There was pressure, the sense of occasion, which would be heightened given that I was bowing out of the Giro, and also by the setting – surrounded by Rome's most famous, ancient landmarks. We flew down from Venice in the morning, ready for a 3.30pm start. On the bus my mood had already darkened as I listened to Shefer gabbling about arrangements for after the stage – basically the logistics of everyone getting home. We had a job to do, a sprint still to contest – that was the priority. It felt as though Shefer couldn't wait to get out of there, which also maybe explained why, until I intervened, everyone had been booked on flights out of Rome that night. To me, this hadn't sat right: it wasn't about celebrating the end of my Giro journey, but rather the adventure we'd all shared over the previous three weeks. OK, we hadn't won anything – yet – but in the space of nearly a month, we'd been through a lot. We'd suffered, we'd laughed, we'd argued, we'd forgiven each other … Fuck, Joe and Gianni had even become friends. These were all things worth celebrating, and so I'd got all of our travel plans put back to the following day, so that we could have a nice meal and drink together.

Fortunately, our other directeur sportif, Stefano Zanini, was still very much focused on the job in hand. He took the pre-stage briefing, with me chipping in with what I knew would be some key non-negotiables. The main one: contrary to what I usually told the guys, what I always said about picking one side of the road and staying there, this was a day and a final kilometre for staying in the middle of the road and letting the two halves of the peloton part in front of us. The lads got it, all nodded, then stepped out of the bus, ready and motivated for one last dance.

The Giro was one race where an old, now nearly extinct tradition still survived: riders from different teams gathering in the hospitality tents a few minutes before the start for a chat and sometimes a coffee. I spotted Ben Swift – 'Swifty' – and sat down. He was riding for INEOS Grenadiers, the same team as G … who appeared over my shoulder, suddenly, even before I was able to ask Swifty about the mood in the camp. We both sat down, and I froze. Several seconds elapsed before I said anything. In fact, before I spoke, tears were welling behind my sunshades.

I couldn't stay silent. But what to say? Eventually, the most obvious words dribbled out.

'I am so, so sorry, mate. I don't know what else to say …'

I glanced across at Swifty and could see that he was also crying. G's response was quintessential G, albeit that his voice was also cracking. 'Well, it's just one of them, innit?'

One day the apocalypse will finally come and swallow us all up, and G'll be sitting there in his Lycra, the last one left, saying, 'Well, it's just one of them, innit?'

My last ever Giro stage was starting in ten minutes – there was barely time to swig down an espresso, never mind get lost in nostalgic rumination. But, later, I'd think about the poignancy of those few seconds and those tears. Fifteen years earlier Italy had been the sort of base camp from which the three of us – G, Swifty and me – all began our ascent of cycling Everest – establishing ourselves as professional cyclists. A tiny British enclave had been created in the fiefdom of the Anglo-Italian former rider Max Sciandri: Quarrata, an unpretentious Tuscan town famed for sofa manufacturing in which we, too, ended up becoming part of the furniture. Both slightly younger than me, in 2006 Swifty and Geraint had been stationed there as part of the British Academy programme under Max's watch. I was racing at Under-23 level, mainly in Germany, still waiting to make the final step up, but fell in love with Tuscany and the town during a training block in early 2006. Eventually, Geraint would move out of the Academy flat, into his place on the main piazza, and I'd move in with him. In a previous book, I likened our previous living arrangement in the Academy's first student-style flats in Manchester to the 1980s British sitcom *The Young Ones*. This, in Quarrata, was a scarcely more sophisticated set-up: not quite '*The Inbetweeners* in Italy' but hardly Stanley Tucci, either. Let's just say that if the walls of the bar underneath our apartment and the hub of town life, Bar Grazia, had ears, they'd be able to tell a few tales. As for the apartment walls, the red wine stains might be still there, like tattoos immortalising the formative years of a Tour de France winner and a Tour de France record holder.

Years later, once we'd all turned pro, I'd end up buying a house in Quarrata. Meanwhile, Swifty, a Yorkshireman, moved to the Isle of Man. The nicest guy in world, Swifty. I'd known not just him but his whole family since we were teenagers. His parents came to every race in their camper van and, over time, became almost my surrogate 'race-day family'. It was never a case of them feeling sorry for this poor Manx lad, who'd come to the mainland on his own, just him and his bike on his ferry. No, they acted like a mum and dad to everyone, and their camper became a kind of open-door clubhouse where everyone could and would congregate. Or, when they'd come with the car, Swifty's mum would open the boot and all manner of toys, sports equipment and cycling kit to keep kids happy or entertained would spill out onto the ground. One summer, I remember, the junior racing scene was gripped by a single obsession: the long overshoes that the big Tour de France stars of the day, Lance Armstrong and Jan Ullrich, had taken to wearing. You couldn't find them for love or money … only Swifty's mum had somehow bought a crate-load, which, at one race, she magically yanked out of the camper van and started to distribute to whoever wanted a pair. The whole northern England kids' cycling community idolised her, so much so that, years later, Swifty had got used to the same greeting from everyone who had known that time and world: 'Eh up, Swifty. How's your mum?'

It all seemed a very long time ago. And yet here we were, in Rome, the three of us together, all hiding tears behind our sunglasses, about to finish a Giro d'Italia that Geraint had nearly won, should have won. And which represented the end of my journey in this race.

I gathered myself. The race started and followed the usual final-stage pattern of an easy first half – the champion elect, in this case Roglič, sipping from a champagne glass and smiling for the cameras – and then a gradual ramping up as we headed towards the finale. The *percorso* ended with six laps of a 13.6-kilometre circuit taking in some of the city's main landmarks, including the Colosseum. While others chatted, swapping congratulations or war stories from the previous two weeks, I used the first few laps to conduct a forensic survey of the road surface in every section of the circuit. In the bus, I'd already laid out the strategy for the last couple of kilometres: that moment where other teams would fan left and right and a pathway would open up through the middle. Before that there were watts to save on every metre of tarmac, every pothole that could be avoided, in every murmur of breeze through the branches of the umbrella pines lining the boulevards.

The lads were doing well. Certainly the best they could. Then, though, as the laps ticked down, teams who had no business being there, no interest in a sprint finish and no

clue how to approach one, started causing havoc. *Fuck's sake.*
At one point I found myself next to Geraint, and, noticing
how no one was bumping and barging his team out of the
line – maybe a privilege of being second on general classification – I asked him if I could just sit on their wheels. He
nodded, of course, then I pushed my luck by asking, tongue
in cheek, if he also fancied leading me out. 'Nah, you're all
right, mate,' he replied this time.

With three kilometres to go I had one team-mate still to
help me: the veteran Spaniard Luis León Sánchez. A multiple Grand Tour stage winner, and maybe a climber, he was a
class act on a bike; following him was like floating on a cloud.
Luis León, though, was by no means a specialist: strong,
smooth, even fearless – all of those things – but he could
take me to the kilometre-to-go kite, then I'd have to fend for
myself. Or so I assumed.

With 2.3 kilometres to go, suddenly, a flash of red to my
right and Luis León's right. 'CAV!' I recognised the voice
and, a split second later, I recognised the pedal stroke and
the silhouette. Fucking Geraint. Fuck me.

I thought he'd do a token pull: 500 metres at most. But
I watched the distance markers on the side of the road spool
past and counted: 600 metres, 700 metres, 800 metres …
He kept going, to – and even for hundreds of metres beyond
– the point where I saw the telltale sign, the trademark little
move that, for as long as I'd known Geraint, signified that he

was really straining, digging as deep as any bike rider could go: the little shift forward onto the nose of the saddle, his toes turning outwards and his heels inwards towards his pedal cranks. We were now almost at the kilometre-to-go flag, yet still he went. A whole kilometre, he'd pulled. I knew Geraint was a hard bastard, but, fuck, this was next level.

Finally, he swung off and Luis León took over – doing just enough to get me nestled where I wanted to be, ready to strike, a few positions off the front. When the Colombian sprinter Fernando Gaviria passed me, leaving clear air behind him, I knew my luck was in: Gaviria always launched his sprints early, which, if you were quicker, made him the perfect lead-out man, the perfect wheel on which to 'squat'. Sure enough, with 250 metres to go, he shot down the right-hand side of the road and I was whistling through his slipstream. With 100 metres to go, Gaviria was done, and all I could see in front of me was clear air all the way to the finish line. After three weeks of near constant grind for no reward, those last few seconds felt effortless, like sprinting into a vacuum. My margin of victory was huge: no one else was even in the photo.

I'd won a lot of races, made a career out of defying the odds, physiologically, the expectations of others and even my own, but rarely had any victory felt so unreal. My last ever day at the Giro, the sun setting over Rome, the Colosseum behind me, me becoming the oldest stage winner in Giro history in

Italy's ancient capital city … it all felt too perfect, too scripted, almost corny. If it was a movie, half of the audience would be wiping their eyes, half rolling them and walking out.

For the second time in a day I was also fighting back the sobs. A few hours earlier, seeing Geraint had been enough to set me off. Now, he appeared in my eye-line again as I made my way back to the podium. We hugged. I held and squeezed him. I might have managed a 'Thank you, mate' or a 'Fucking hell, G …' but, just as I had been before the start, really, once again, I was lost for words.

Fucking Geraint. Fuck me.

CHAPTER 8

Whatever my sense of disorientation and disassociation in the minutes after crossing the line – as though Ridley Scott could appear at any moment and announce that my *Gladiator* remake needed a grittier ending – there was nothing like a bit of petty team politics to snap me back to reality.

The podium ceremony done, the tears all dried, I arrived back at the team bus just as arrangements were being discussed for the evening's celebration. Stefano Zanini wanted to know what the plan was … whereupon an awkward silence descended, and panicked glances were shot back and forth between riders. Eventually, Gianni Moscon spoke. 'Well, we – the riders – have got a table booked at a restaurant. When we asked a few days ago, we were told that nothing was happening on the last night …'

Zanini looked taken aback. I was embarrassed, mortified, so much so that I offered to call the owner of the restaurant, a friend of mine, to ask whether he could expand the table from 12 to … 20 or 30-odd. Hearing this, Moscon piped up again, in Italian this time, to Zanini. 'No! You didn't want to do anything, so we're not changing our plans ...'

For a couple of minutes it got very heated. I was cringing, didn't know what to do or say ... Finally, an hour or two later, at the hotel, the lads insisted: we were going to enjoy our night, as planned, and the management could make their own arrangements. I came down the stairs into the lobby, all dressed up, and could see them in the hotel restaurant, chomping on pasta and drinking cheap wine. 'Guilty' doesn't even begin to cover it.

This aside, our night ended up being everything we'd envisaged and hoped for. It was the perfect celebration of a three-week road trip, the kind only the life of a pro cyclist can provide: the most random bunch of young men, from all four corners of the world, team-mates yet in some cases barely even acquainted, bundled onto a bus and told to do a lap of Italy, covering half of the distance on their bikes. After the meal, we went on to the 'official' end-of-Giro party at a nightclub. There, at one point, I looked over at Joe Dombrowski and Gianni Moscon, chatting away like lifelong pals, and – honest to god – thought to myself that was the biggest win of our whole race, way over and above what had happened that afternoon.

Maybe at the time I just hadn't quite fully appreciated the poignancy of that last Giro win. Or the extent to which others couldn't quite fathom how I'd done it. I hadn't won all season, they'd say, and even during the Giro I'd been in the mix for a stage win only a couple of times. How was it possible that – faced with the likelihood of a resounding anti-climax after 16 career stage wins and a 15-year love affair with this race – I'd somehow pulled this off? Aligned the planets to the point that my boyhood friend who had been cruelly denied 24 hours earlier, was riding for a different team – and with whom I'd shared an apartment in Italy, for fuck's sake – appeared magically over my shoulder with two kilometres to go to give me a chariot-ride to victory? With the fucking Colosseum behind us?!

As much as I generally had little time for overwrought media narratives, this was one occasion where, later, I could at least acknowledge that it seemed almost implausibly poetic, typical of a rider – yours truly – who, as far as the media was concerned, specialised in such melodrama. In fairness, some commentators also pointed out that the victory had underscored something else: how, among whatever other talents and I abilities I'd demonstrated over the years, I had proven once again that I belonged in a small category of 'big game players'. That all of the symbolism was one thing – a beautiful storyline – but that, in the midst of it, and maybe because rather than in spite of the extra pressure the context created, I'd somehow delivered. As the Americans say, I'd come up clutch.

All of which raised the obvious question: how? Not just how I'd done it here but also time and time again during my career? Not wishing to compare myself with arguably the greatest sportsman of all time (!) ... it was a question that Michael Jordan often got asked, particularly after his most iconic 'clutch' moment, against the Cleveland Cavaliers in game five of the 1989 NBA playoffs. With three seconds to go and his team, the Chicago Bulls, trailing by one point in what was the deciding game of the series, Jordan, who was battling sickness, received the ball, took two steps forward then hit a jump shot which dropped in off the back rim literally on the final buzzer. The moment became so famous, so representative of Jordan's career, that it was, and still is, known to every American sports fan simply as 'The Shot'.

When he was asked later about how he retained the mental clarity and physical control to execute at times like those, when the stakes were highest, Jordan said, 'If you have doubt or concern about a shot, or feel the "pressure" of that shot, it's because you haven't practised it enough. The only way to relieve that pressure is to build your fundamentals, practise them over and over, so when game breaks down, you can handle anything that transpires.'

Another Jordan quote that I can identify with is 'I've never lost a game, I just ran out of time.' This, to me, tells you that he saw his career as a process of constant refinement, and his greatest moments as a by-product of that hard labour, not some supernatural power that he magically harnessed when the pressure was on. Again, not ever wanting to put myself in the vicinity of the same pedestal as Jordan, this was how I'd also explain my own ability to deliver when it seemed to matter most. Countless times in my career I've been described as 'emotional', and that characterisation was accurate in the sense that, yes, I was naturally demonstrative in showing joy or anger or frustration, particularly in races. Often, though, I think people would look at that tendency to wear my heart on my sleeve and assume that was the secret of my capacity to come up clutch; a sort of resonance with the higher emotional wavelength of major events or critical moments, as though only when a race or situation evoked intense feelings could all of my powers be 'switched on'. In fact, the opposite was almost true.

Maybe the most fundamental misapprehension was that I must enjoy the pressure. Sorry to burst some bubbles, but that just wasn't true; before that last stage in Rome, for example, I wasn't relishing the fact that I hadn't yet won a stage and now had one shot left. I felt that weight as much as anyone would. I was nervous. Edgy. Not to the extent that I thought my world would fall apart if I didn't win on my last day at the Giro, but anxious nonetheless. I just didn't crumble under that pressure. That was the difference. And I didn't and don't crumble because my process is so well practised and so meticulous.

For me it's always been hard to analyse ... because the instincts that make me commit to that process are to some extent second nature. Maybe in that respect I am unique or at least unusual, and perhaps I have my parents to thank for two totally contradictory sides to my personality and approach to things: one, sometimes excessively emotional, entirely from my mum; the other, completely dispassionate, from my dad. If I were to psychoanalyse myself – with absolutely zero credentials to do so – I would say this dichotomy is exactly why it can often look as though, with me, a storm is raging on the surface, but there are still waters underneath.

Jordan also hints at the distinction between the process itself and the process *leading to* that process. In other words, it's relatively easy, at any given moment, to identify and concentrate on all the micro-actions or variables you need to master to produce a good outcome, but it's usually too late if you only start when you feel the spotlight on your shoulders. There was no better illustration of this than Rome and the Giro. For days I'd been watching the breakout Italian sprint star of the Giro, Jonathan Milan, flogging himself to try to hold on to the main peloton for as long as possible on hilly and mountainous stages. He wasn't the only sprinter doing it – needlessly depleting their energy stores on days when there was nothing more to gain than a wider margin of survival. Two weeks into the race, those guys were all paying for their efforts, whereas I, relatively speaking, had mental and physical energy to spare. You can see the moment when these guys' heads go in a three-week race, when you know they're beaten; for Jonathan Milan, it was in the Dolomites a couple of days before the end, when, surrounded by the walking dead at that point, Moscon and I rode away from the gruppetto and back to the main peloton. Seeing that, I'm fairly certain that Milan already knew that he wasn't beating me in Rome.

During the stage itself, yes, there'd been some good fortune – for example, Geraint's, ahem, intervention. I couldn't have foreseen that. Equally, I'd been maniacal about saving energy on every one of the laps, and also gathering the 'intelligence' I needed to have a clear plan for the key moments. By this point in my career I'd done hundreds, in fact thousands, of sprints, and it'd been demonstrated to me over and over again that having to make decisions on the fly cost nervous energy. Some element of improvisation was unavoidable – for example jumping onto Geraint's wheel as he flew by me. But going off script was just another way to unbalance you, leave you even more vulnerable to unhelpful emotion. Often the adrenaline – unleashed by fear or nerves or excitement – would kick off a bargaining process in your mind, and that was where doubt would insert itself. If, though, a lot of the key decisions had already been made ahead of time, when the nervous system was still calm, I found that the challenge of simply executing was a lot easier than the internal negotiation you had to do to keep the questions at bay.

Some riders simply learned over the course of a career, through trial and a lot of error, how important it was to 'do your homework'. It had always been part of my method – and, in fact, over the years, some of my advantage had been eroded as it became easier to take the same forensic approach.

Team Sky were often credited with all manner of innovations – 'marginal' gains or not – but they didn't invent everything. In 2010, riding for HTC, I had a rotten start to the Tour, so much so that, after three botched sprints, my long-time soigneur decided that I needed to relax by forsaking my nightly massage in favour of a couple of gin and tonics. That may well have helped … but so, equally, did doubling down on the prep work. That year my lead-out man Mark Renshaw and I had discovered the then pretty rudimentary Google Street View (launched in 2007). Before some stages, we'd spend hours in our rooms debating which lines to take, mentally noting landmarks on the roadside that we could use as our cue-points, creating a perfect 3D mental map of where we'd be in a few hours. It maybe says a lot about how and why I finally ended my losing streak at that Tour that I remember the satellite images of the closing kilometre displayed on my laptop screen more clearly than I remember the actual finish and the moment I crossed the line.

Fast forward to 2024 and the same attention to detail has become de rigueur in the peloton, not just because riders and directeurs sportif are desperately looking for an edge but also because they're terrified of being caught out, exposed as the only ones not harnessing the now widely available technology. Pre-race briefings in team buses used to last ten minutes; now they sometimes go on for half an hour, between PowerPoint presentations and forensic analysis of the latest weather bulletins. Teams have experts in every domain ... but often what's missing is the actual riders' intuition or ingenuity. I was constantly, obsessively thinking about how to get an edge. Sometimes equipment suppliers didn't listen because I didn't look or sound like a nerd, didn't always know the correct terminology, but early in my career, especially, there were countless occasions when my 'feedback' led to real, material gains. The chunky stem I insisted that Shimano make for me in 2009, for example, for better leverage in sprints – widely mocked at the time but now ubiquitous on modern bikes; the plastic cover over the air vents in my helmet at the 2011 Worlds; my insistence that I wouldn't use electronic gear shifting in 2011 until Specialized found a better place for the battery than on the downtube – and my suggestion, which they finally implemented, that it go in the seatpost. Admittedly, there were also ideas that gained a bit of traction but didn't necessarily stand the test of time or proved unworkable. Renting a camping car to sleep in at stage races was one that came to me after seeing my mate Cal Crutchlow's set-up at MotoGP races. I mentioned it to Dave Brailsford, who then tried it with Team Sky and Richie Porte at the Giro d'Italia, only for the UCI to step in and say that it was against the rules. Dave ended up keeping the camping car, hiring a driver and using it as his own mobile home when he went to races. So I suppose you win some, you lose some.

My mind was constantly whirring, constantly working. At the start of my career, I got the sense that this was why a lot of equipment sponsors were in the sport – to mine the riders' insight and experience. Later, it generally felt more like you were given kit as a fait accompli, that conversations with kit suppliers were more about them selling you their product and ideas. Often, I'd be left scratching my head. We were obliged to use their stuff, per our contracts. They didn't particularly want to hear what we thought: they wanted us to win with their products so they could tell the world about it on Instagram.

But, again, for me, delivering under pressure was a by-product of looking after the minutiae. And, also, willingly accepting that pressure. I'd seen so many riders folding when opportunities presented themselves, not seizing their chance. It was a refrain I'd heard so many times: 'Oh, I could win but the team never backs me …' This could also have been me at the start of my career with T-Mobile, when the decision-makers in the team were, shall we say, divided on my poten-tial. In lead-out drills at my first training camps, in the winter of 2006–7, I'd been clearly faster that the team's other up-and-coming sprinter, the German André Greipel, yet Greipel was the nominated sprinter for our first stage race together a few weeks later, the Étoile de Bessèges. When I inadvertently dropped him in the lead-out on stage one, André seethed but ultimately he'd squandered an oppor-tunity. A few weeks later, in contrast, I got my shot at Scheldeprijs and took it, winning the race. The same pattern would repeat itself again and again over the next couple of years: me seizing the big moments, André sometimes freezing. He'd go on to have an incredible career, winning 11 stages at the Tour de France, but he had to leave T-Mobile to get first dibs on the most prestigious races.

André certainly figured it out himself in the end whereas others simply decide that they don't want to stand in the heat. A lead-out rider who looks fast enough to sprint for himself is a common test case. The last man in my train for several years at QuickStep, Fabio Sabatini, was a good example. I once asked him why he appeared to have shelved all personal ambition when, clearly, he had the speed to at least compete for victories himself. He said that it was simple: he'd given it a go early in his career and recognised pretty quickly that he became half the rider as 'the' guy. He'd had the intelligence or pragmatism to realise that he could have a longer, less stressful and maybe even more lucrative career sacrificing himself for others than by trying to become a star.

· · ·

Whatever ingredients had gone into the Giro win, whatever factors accounted for how and why I had – once again – come up clutch, it had provided the perfect microcosm of what hopefully now awaited me: not the triumphant ending to a single, 3-week race but to a 17-year career. At the Giro I'd 'left it' until the last day, the last finish line, with the most grandiose setting imaginable. The Tour was, figuratively speaking, all of this writ large – the ultimate test, if one was needed, of my capacity to produce the remarkable and even unprecedented when required.

The 2023 Tour was to start in Spain or, to be more precise, in Bilbao in the Basque Country. I'd taken a risk in choosing the notoriously dangerous, five-day Ster ZLM Tour in the Netherlands in mid-June as my final preparation race. This was the ideal place to sharpen up, get some zip in the legs – providing you could avoid crashes. My goal wasn't to win or even test myself in the sprints, so I could afford to steer well clear of any unfolding chaos, anything that looked sketchy. At the end of week it was mission accomplished: no injuries, no illness, form and confidence in tact.

I travelled to Spain with an outlook scarcely any different from other years. The work was done, the engine built. There was no guarantee of success but I had no great regrets, either. It would be my fourteenth Tour but I certainly wasn't blasé – and not only because it would also be my last. Over all the years, through all my success, I'd never lost my sense of perspective around what this race represented and the privilege of being on the start line. There had been many moments over the previous few years when cycling had felt very much like a job or duty, when it had taken something or someone to remind me that, in spite of everything, I was still living my dream. But no such memory jog or sense check had ever been required at the Tour. Whatever fears and pressures I carried into the Tour in any year, they were outweighed and eclipsed by my sense of exhilaration and privilege at taking part in the sport's greatest event, a race whose reach and impact in fact dwarfed that sport's other component parts.

What had changed this time was my attitude to the ultimate goal: that of winning my thirty-fifth stage. At other points in my career, I'd gone in with a sense of 'win or be damned', a heavy feeling that a stage victory was an obligation more than a target. Here, now, in Bilbao, the message that Alexander Vinokourov had spelled out to me in the winter and on multiple occasions since still rang clearly and comfortingly in my ears: all we could do was *try*. Within those three letters were contained two efforts – one lasting several months before the Tour, and one concentrated within 21 days or, more accurately, a few critical split seconds in certain stages, when a right or wrong decision could alter my legacy for ever. That first, longer effort had been accomplished. Now came the shorter but more intense part – but again an 'effort' or 'attempt' was all it was. Repeating this to myself made me feel instantly lighter.

We'd also made a huge amount of progress as a team since the start of year. I could never accuse Vino of not backing me. He'd bought – not been given by a sponsor – new wheels when I said that what we had were good and solid but not fast. He'd also listened and ultimately acquiesced when I made the case for recruiting my old lead-out man Mark Renshaw as a directeur sportif who'd specialise in studying and planning for the flatter finishes where I'd have a chance. Renshaw arrived at our hotel for the first few nights of the Tour, just outside Vitoria-Gasteiz, with data and videos and good ideas coming out of his ears. He'd be a calming influence, someone who knew me and knew the sort of diligence and commitment I expected from those around me. As regards riders, no one in the team would be offended to hear me say that we had to make a little go a long way. Cees Bol would be my 'last' man but not strictly speaking my lead-out man: even to get me to the kilometre-to-go mark, he'd have to do the work of two riders. From there, it'd then be on me, my savvy and my ability to squat on wheels to find someone, an 'opponent' from whose wheel I could launch my sprint at or just before the 200-metre sign.

One thing I could be sure of was that, for my final send-off in a Tour de France, the last Grand Départ I'd ever experience as a rider, I'd be treated to an incredible atmosphere in the Basque Country. Everyone who knows anything about professional cycling will tell you that, if no fans are as knowledgeable and steeped in the culture of the sport as the Belgians, the most passionate, without any doubt, are the Basques. I'd have this underlined to me throughout the three stages we'd be spending in the region before crossing into France, but, before that, even the team presentation two nights before stage one had felt magical, inebriating. The backdrop was Bilbao's most famous landmark and tourist attraction: the Frank Gehry-designed Guggenheim Museum, less a building than a landscape of its own, sprawling towards the Nervión river and the mountains beyond. I heard the Basque fans' cheers echo off the museum's titanium walls when the announcer invited me onto the stage, reeling off my career highlights in Basque, French and finally English. Before leaving for Spain I'd promised myself to take in every instant, every sight and every sound of my last Tour, let them soak through my senses, into every cell, impregnating my memory with as much as it could preserve of what would soon be my wild former life. Fuck, I was forcing myself to enjoy – or at least *try* to enjoy – even the most annoying bits. Perfect example: the photo-call with the Tour's social media team, in which every year you'd be asked to stand in front of a camera in full racing kit and 'Do some-ziiing funny for ze camera, Mark.' In every other year all I'd *actually* wanted to do was cringe. Now, on my cue, I was prancing and dancing and giving thumbs-ups like I was in the Disney Club and not a world-class sporting event.

The fun and games would of course all end the moment we rolled out from Bilbao on stage one. I braced myself, remembering 2021, when I hadn't raced the Tour for three years and the first half-hour on stage one felt like a fever dream on fast forward. Now, two years later, Christian Prudhomme waved his flag to signal the start of the Tour … but, over the next couple of hours, that feeling of overwhelm, of being in over my head, never came. There are days when you have to grind, and days when you can 'stroke' or 'caress' the pedals. This, happily, was one of the latter.

The goal for each of the first two days was very simple: get to the stage finish inside the time limit while expending as little energy as possible. The Basque Country is a land of contrasts – an unruly corner of Atlantic Ocean overlooked by sharply rising, pine-cloaked hills and mountains, like giant traffic cones hidden under an enormous green quilt. I'd hardly ever raced in the region – mainly because the terrain turns sprinter-unfriendly as soon as you venture more than a couple of kilometres from the coast. Stage one had a profile like a crocodile's dental X-ray. On the climbs, I stuck to my own pace, or rather the power number, the wattage, that I knew I could maintain. I'd get dropped going up, then rejoin the peloton on the way down, or in the valley before the next climb, never losing heart or composure. In fact, the biggest test that day was of my patience with modern racing. Yep, that again: a peloton hammering away, led by UAE, apparently trying to keep the breakaway within striking distance, then suddenly allowing the gap to go out again and repeating the whole senseless cycle. I had my own plan so could stick to that, regardless, but it didn't stop me getting frustrated. Or thinking, as I had at the Giro, that this was no longer my place, no longer the sport I'd known for most of my career.

It did turn into a memorable day for British cycling … but that was thanks to the Yates twins, Adam and Simon. Although now riding for different teams, they got away, on their own, and finished first and second respectively in Bilbao.

Meanwhile, I was cruising in several minutes behind, flanked by screaming Basque fans and smiling from ear to ear. Every year, they'd descend on the Pyrenees, just a couple of hours' drive away, but I'd never seen them in such concentration. Every rider got the same messianic reception – and yet somehow it also felt personal, as though they'd all schlepped up the mountain and spent the whole day waiting with their beers and picnics just to see *you*. Theirs was pure, unreserved support and positivity. Occasionally, during the Tour, among the encouraging voices at the roadside, I'd hear the odd 'Come on, Cav, move your arse' in a British accent and find myself fixating on it for the rest of the stage, even muttering under my breath, 'What the fuck was that?' Here, I just wanted to climb off and give every last one of them a hug.

Stage two was a similar sawtooth, with the same brilliant fans and a finish on the seafront in San Sebastián. We were then crossing into France for what we be my first chance of the race – a billiard table of a third stage to Bayonne. The lads all did their jobs but the last few kilometres were carnage. I ended up in the middle of the chaos on the finishing straight, just happy to stay upright. Jasper Philipsen won, I got sixth. The same social media managers I'd entertained with my poses for the pre-race photos then put a smile on my face later in the day by posting a curious statistic: I'd been the rider to hit the highest top speed in the sprint.

This augured well, and another opportunity presented itself immediately. Again, no major climbs – just a few gentle ripples as we headed into Armagnac country and a finishing circuit on the Nogaro motor-racing track. We'd gone through all the key points on the bus in the morning briefing. Among them, a roundabout with around four kilometres to go that we *had* to take on the left side. First mistake: we went to the right, not left, and lost 20 positions in the peloton. Next mistake, after mighty pulls from Yevgeniy Fedorov and Cees Bol to get me back into contention, my decision to sit on Mads Pedersen's wheel and trust his habit of launching early. In theory, it was ideal – especially into a headwind. In practice, for some reason, Mads stayed rooted, and, as I waited, Mathieu van der Poel whistled past me on my left with Philipsen on his wheel. And third mistake, or at least misfortune: not mine but my team-mate Luis León Sánchez's. He crashed on the last corner and was already on his way home with a broken collarbone.

I'd finished one place higher than the previous day, in fifth. Clearly I was in the mix, in the hunt. Equally, though, two chances had already slipped by, and another one wouldn't come for a few days, because we were heading into the mountains. Two brutal stages over infamous Pyrenean passes now awaited. I was confident in my form but, equally, we could take nothing for granted. Cees and Gianni Moscon would stick with me – and it was up to all of us to stick to a plan. Above all, it was essential to remember that even if your legs didn't let you down, your ego might. I'd seen it so many times with other sprinters – and I saw it again now: as the road reared up on the first major Pyrenean climb in the Tour, the Col de Soudet, and we calmly climbed at the pace we knew we could sustain, a few hundred metres up the road I saw other sprinters arching their backs and rocking all over their bikes to stay with the main peloton. Once again, I watched them in total bafflement and, also, amusement and delight, because I knew that the next time we sprinted they'd pay for these efforts. Long before that, in fact often within a couple of minutes or a hundred metres, they'd also be boomeranging back towards me and, often, soon struggling to hold even my wheel. I must confess that at moments like these whatever camaraderie existed in the 'sprinters' union' could briefly give way to something resembling Schadenfreude and even a spot of gamesmanship. Now, when I saw the man who QuickStep had picked instead of me in 2022, Fabio Jakobsen, first giving everything to hold on longer than me, then sliding back towards us and finally barely hanging on to our wheels, I couldn't resist: suddenly my demeanour was that of a village postman on a sunny spring morning, every rider in the vicinity a potential conversation partner. That was, except Fabio, who by that point would have been wheezing too hard for us to properly 'catch up'.

You're disappointed in me, I know. But you don't win 30-odd stages of the Tour de France by being Paddington Bear.

Anyway, I survived the two Pyrenean stages. So did Fabio, incidentally, despite finishing dead last and second to last. Next stop was Bordeaux, a city that brought back happy memories. In 2010 I'd won the fourth of my five stages in that edition there. You could broadly throw a blanket over four seasons from 2009 to 2012 and say that, in those years, I was at the peak of my craft, the pinnacle of my physical capabilities. That particular Tour was fruitful, and, with the sport still slowly lurching out of its darkest era, its established GC stars almost all tainted by association with the recent past, I'd quickly established myself as the biggest show in town. I was authentic, brash, fast and impossible to ignore – 'pure Hollywood' said the media, certainly that day in Bordeaux, when the biggest film stars of the day, Cameron Diaz and *Mission Impossible*'s Tom Cruise, visited the Tour on their day off from promoting *Knight and Day*, and congratulated me on the podium.

Mission impossible was exactly how some of the same scribes might have described my quest for a thirty-fifth stage win 13 years later, but I was feeling bullish. I'd won in Paris four times, Châteauroux three times, Valence twice, so clearly there was such a thing as 'horses for courses' – or at least cities. The stage itself would head north across relentlessly flat roads bisecting dense pine forests – 'les Landes' as the region's known. Days like this, with no significant climbs but the threat of wind, were always tense, and this was no exception. The pace was so fast, the anxiety level in the bunch so high, that at certain moments in the race I found myself fighting two battles: one to hold my position and the wheel in front of me and the other with an inner monologue: *Fuck this. It's your last Tour. Just pull to the side of the road and get off* …

Of course I'd heard a variation of this hundreds of times before. Every rider had. We were all experts in denial – of pain, of appetite, of gravity. Of what would be the wise decision to jack it all in. And so on I went, trying to block out everything, including the nagging feeling that, after a puncture and wheel change earlier in the stage, my chain wasn't quite right, not perfectly slotting into the gears. Just a slight noise, a 'brrrmm', a friction so scarcely perceptible that I thought I might be imagining it. Ordinarily, I'd have changed wheels or bikes, just to be sure, but in the last 50 kilometres that wasn't an option. *Deny. Shut it out. Race head on. Focus, Cav, for fuck's sake focus.*

• • •

The run-in was broadly similar to 2010 but not a copy-paste. We'd identified a few key points or punctuation marks in the last ten kilometres – roadworks where the lane narrowed, roundabouts or bridges – and before each one we'd try to move up and then give ourselves a moment to ease off. I run the tape in my head now and I'm back there, in the 'flow' – the wheels on the tarmac, the bike and my body moving as one, the pictures spooling through my field of vision. Right. Down. Around a roundabout. Under a bridge. Up. Straight. Down. Under the tunnel and into the finish straight …

With 500 metres to go I'm on Cees's wheel on the right-hand side of the road but he's stuck behind a wall of bodies. We're fucked, done ... only then everything and everyone in front starts to edge ever so slightly to the left of the road. There's a corridor up the right and I go for it. But the swarm of riders in front of me starts drifting to that side too. I'm accelerating, just need the two Uno-X riders blocking my path to give me an inch, a glimpse, then I'll find a way. If they don't move, I'm fucked – I'll have to brake and lose all my speed. I let out a 'Whooaaa ...' but don't even have time to work out who or what I'm shouting at before a Bahrain rider appears from behind us on my left and bounces both of the Uno-X guys to the left.

Now, out of nowhere, I see clear daylight. A fucking miracle. It's meant to be. This is it, Cav.

Suddenly, I've got a wheel. A good one: Biniam Girmay. But he's moving left with all the others and with 200 metres to go the whole right side opens up, like someone's teasing open the pearly gates. It's early but it's time, the moment. I've got momentum, so I crank hard and I'm a bullet out of a barrel – twice the speed of all of them, even Jasper Philipsen, whose green jersey is the last blur in the corner of my eyeline as I whistle towards the finish line.

Unfortunately, a split second later, my legs are turning faster than I can manage and I hear that noise every cyclist knows – of the chain skipping across sprockets only not quite making it, getting stuck in between, in a sort of mechanical purgatory. Fuck. I instinctively sit down, the power draining from my legs – just for a second, but at 65 kilometres per hour that's enough, more than enough. Click, my chain is back where it should be, in the 11-tooth sprocket. So I stand up. Click, back up to the 12. Fatal. I look down, but by the time I look up again that blur of dark green – Philipsen – has reappeared. He is full size now, full focus – no longer a fly on my rear windscreen but a rival about to steal my dream.

Fifty metres to go. Click. Rattle. Another look down. Fuck. Game over. Second place. Fuck.

I rolled through the finish line, through the journalists and fans who had spilled onto the road, around another gaggle of reporters who had gathered outside our bus. Climbed the steps of the bus, sat down, buried my head in my hands. Fuck! It doesn't pay to look for scapegoats in the heat of the moment, and, here, in any case, suddenly I became oddly calm. I can only liken the feeling to waking from a nightmare or at least the deepest of sleeps. The occasion was huge, the misfortune and especially its timing catastrophic, yet my emotions seemed out of sync with what had just occurred. A fair while later that evening, we'd deduce from photos of the bike that my chain had been slightly bent, its links twisted, possibly during the stage or even before. That year we'd had 'after-market' modifications to our rear derailleurs as part of a team sponsorship agreement. They'd now have to be discarded. Also, no more mid-stage wheel swaps like the one I'd needed that day. From now on, only full bike changes. There's always a reason, however subtle or difficult to locate. But what good would it do now to be angry? The moment, the chance had passed. And if I'd somehow got myself to 34 stage wins in the Tour de France over the previous decade and a half, it had been thanks to a resolute determination to look forwards and never back. That starts with focusing on what's in your power to avoid preventable mistakes.

In this case that meant focusing immediately on the next day. Limoges – another chance. We'd finished there before, but this was a different finale – harder, with a stiffer climb to the finish line. So, a slim chance, a day to play it by ear, see how I felt later, as the kilometres ticked down. The sun was also blazing, and so we sat towards the back of the pack, well away from the scrap for position. There, you spend more energy physically, sprinting out of corners to close gaps, but you compensate that with moments where you can, relatively speaking, rest your mind and your legs.

And herein lies one of the dangers: when you take the path of least stress, you can also switch off. Another is that the peloton slows and accelerates in waves, and the ripples get bigger and more dangerous the further back you're sitting in the group. In other words, if towards the front of the peloton someone touches their brakes for whatever reason, there might be twenty guys behind him who also have to touch their brakes, and every one of those twenty could either brake a tiny fraction too hard or too softly, too early or too late. We're talking minuscule under- or over-corrections, yet sometimes that's all it takes for wheels to touch or get snagged in a derailleur and bring someone down.

Which, out of nowhere, 61 kilometres from the finish, is what happened now. I don't even know exactly whose wheel I hit, whether it was he who'd slowed too much, whether I'd misjudged the speed or the space in front. All I can remember is that suddenly I looked down and saw a front wheel that was inert, locked or blocked – and then in the next instant I was being flipped over the handlebars. I thudded into the tarmac. Went to sit up … and that's when the pain came: a searing, burning sensation in my right shoulder. I looked up and saw Gianni Moscon, who over the previous months had become a kind of guardian angel, never leaving my side. After the row over dinner on the last night of the Giro, the team management had said they didn't want him at the Tour; I'd dug my heels in, insisting that he had to get picked, that we didn't have anyone in the roster who would look after me like he did. Now, I knew that within a minute or two he'd have to smile apologetically, say he was sorry, turn his bike to face down the route and pedal off without me. Meanwhile, I'd be helped into an ambulance and driven away from the Tour.

Before the Tour doctor slid the door shut I sat on the back seat, staring into the distance. Of course I was also being filmed and photographed. Later, people would talk to me about the poignancy of the image – how it was both tragic yet maybe also fitting that this was how I'd be ending my career: wounded, forced from the battlefield rather than defeated. My career had been defined as much by adversity as it had by success, people said. Somehow it seemed heart-breaking but apt.

None of this was on my mind. I knew my Tour de France was over, but I couldn't think beyond that. I'd been here before – crashing out of the Tour, in 2014 and 2017. The feeling was exactly the same. A hollowness, a void which only later would fill with emotions. Anger. Sadness. Regret. For now I was preoccupied with only one thing – and that was how to dull the physical pain. Fortunately, the race doctor would do that for me – or give me something that could: a green inhaler containing the powerful painkiller methoxyflurane.

The journey to the hospital was, nonetheless, long and uncomfortable. There are designated hospitals for every stage, usually one closer to the start and one close to the finish – and for some reason now they were taking me the 150 kilometres or so to the one near the start. Peta and the kids had arrived two days earlier and now, when one of the old QuickStep doctors texted her to say that I'd crashed, she had to bundle everything and everyone into the hire car and drive more than two hours to the south.

An X-ray confirmed what I pretty much already knew: I'd broken my collarbone. But of course this wasn't the news that everyone was waiting on, or an answer to the question everyone was asking: did this mean the end, retirement, as I'd promised … or would I now reconsider, give it one last shot? Already, that night, Peta said exactly those words to me – 'Ah, well, you have to go again now …' – but the effects of the painkillers were too inebriating for me to know whether she was being serious. I remember being dismissive, saying, 'Nah, forget it,' but also lacking clarity in my thoughts and therefore conviction in my words.

Vasi called that evening and also planted the seed. He claims now that he knew that night, from talking to me on the phone, that I was giving it one more go. He'd just agreed a deal to leave Soudal–QuickStep and come to Astana as head of performance in 2024, possibly to work alongside me in a management role. But now we were talking about me still being a rider and coming back to the Tour. Or so he says. He even reckons we talked about recruiting new riders for the lead-out train – Michael Mørkøv and Tim Declercq. Says that it was obvious then. And that he gave me the whole spiel about not sitting on the couch in 20 years and wishing I'd tried one more time, but that Peta and the kids also had to give me their blessing. He claims that two days later he sent me a draft 2024 race programme … Who knows, his memory might be a lot better than mine. Either that or, not for the first time, Vasi is demonstrating why, ever since antiquity, the Greeks have been admired and envied for their theatre and storytelling!

One call I definitely remember from that night was from Cal Crutchlow, the former MotoGP rider and one of my best mates for over a decade. I'd first met Cal in a group ride on the Isle of Man, where he was living. We hit it off pretty much straight away, probably because we had two big things in common – one, our job as professional sportsmen and, two, the fact that we don't give our trust away very easily. Cal's not always the easiest guy to pin down – but when you need him he's there, with whatever you need, in an instant. Now, true to form, he called to say that he had already spoken to the orthopaedic surgeon in Manchester who'd operated on my shoulder in 2014, got me an appointment and arranged a private jet to fly me and the family back to the UK.

We'd leave the next day. First, we had to collect my stuff from the team hotel – another 200 kilometres back north – and also say my goodbyes. When I walked through the door one of the first faces I saw was that of the team manager, Vino. He greeted me with a huge, warm smile and an order: 'Now we have to go again.' Once again, as with Peta, I bowed my gaze, shook my head and said, 'Nah, that's it. It's all over.' It wouldn't be the last time I got the same comments, the same cajoling that night, as my team-mates consoled me, and I shared a beer with the staff. But every time my response was the same. Nope. I was done.

Later, nearly two years later, in fact, Netflix's Tour de France docu-series *Unchained* showed an, ahem, excerpt from another conversation with Peta and the kids at breakfast the following morning. Most who watched the scene would have taken from it that my arm didn't need much twisting, or that I'd already made up my mind. In it, Peta suggests no one would care or object to me effectively reneging on my decision to retire, and, even if they did, in her words, 'Who gave a fuck?' The viewer neither sees nor hears me disagree, but, in reality, it'd be over a month before I truly made up my mind.

First there were plenty of practicalities to occupy my thoughts. The operation – which required a bone graft from my hip to fix the break, where a pin from my 2014 surgery, after my Tour crash, had been dislodged. A trip to the last stage of the Tour in Paris and another pep-talk from Vino, about how I 'couldn't finish like this', which I again batted away. The premiere of my documentary, *Never Enough*, in London. My first time back on a bike, indoors, on Zwift, on 25 July, with my hip twisted like a pretzel and my groin howling. A trip to the Natural History Museum in London with the kids. A holiday in Sardinia. The first rides outdoors there, again like a fucking pedalling pretzel …

Over two or three weeks that August, it's true that, slowly, my feelings started to shift – or at least evolve. I must have been entertaining the idea because I called Michael Mørkøv and Tim Declercq about leaving Soudal and coming to Astana … without knowing whether I'd be a rider in 2024, on the management team or just a mate helping Vino out.

I'd also have the odd good day on the bike, and start to wonder again. Invariably, though, these would be followed by two or three days when I couldn't turn the cranks and the notion of racing another season seemed ridiculous.

And so it went for a few weeks. I carried on training simply out of duty, because I was still, officially, a professional bike rider until the end of the year. I continued to have the odd good day. Maybe it was after one of them that the whole family was having dinner one night. All around the oval table in our house in Essex, and suddenly one of the kids mentioned something – maybe a holiday or an outing – that they wanted to do the following year. I can remember instinctively, matter-of-factly responding that, well, we could finally do that, because Daddy wasn't going to be a professional bike rider any more.

I'll also never forget catching Casper's eye as I said it, and watching his expression change. He looked crestfallen. Within a second or two, in fact, I could see tears welling in his eyes.

It was horrible. I shuddered.

'So you still want Daddy to be a bike rider?' I said, turning to face him. He nodded, his bottom lip quivering. I then turned to the others and said we'd put it to a vote: who thought that Daddy should carry on racing his bike?

The vote was unanimous, except for Astrid, who, at the age of one, was allowed to abstain.

I took a deep breath. 'All right then,' I said finally. 'Guess I'm giving it one more go.'

A few days later, Peta and I took our eldest daughter, Delilah, to get her ears pierced in central London. I'd been planning to get the kids' initials tattooed on my arm for a while, and this seemed like a good time to do it. But I also added something else: a little red triangle on the inside of my forearm, like the kilometre 'kite' – the *'Flamme Rouge'* or 'Red Flame' that signifies the start of the final kilometre in a bike race. For almost half of my life, this and the final thousand metres of bike races had been a huge part of my life, and what defined me in my sport. They were my arena, my canvas. But the tattoo was also, of course, a metaphor for what I was now taking on: a last push, to which I'd have to commit fully, without compromise, and knowing that there would be no second to dwell or repeat or re-engineer – only the inexorable approach of the finish line. Over the next few months, every time that I'd be tempted to finish a session a few minutes early, cut a few kilometres off a ride or skip a last interval, all I'd have to do was look down, see the red triangle on my left arm and be reminded: last kilometre, last push, all in. No compromises and no regrets.

That was the message and the manifesto. Now it was time, the last time, to get this thing done.

CHAPTER 9

There was no big announcement. No press conference to retract the press conference I'd given at the Giro a few months earlier. But my retirement from my impending retirement was sealed from the moment Vino convinced me to race the Tour of Turkey at the end of 2023, not to round out the season but effectively as my first real preparation race for 2024. Don't worry about results; in fact, don't even bother sprinting, he said. In the mountain stages all I had to do was find my pace, find my group, and cruise in. Lay the first foundation stone for July 2024 in October 2023. Plenty of people didn't have much time for Vino, and didn't think I should either, but this was why, in my book, he was a brilliant manager; what he was telling me now was exactly what I needed to hear.

We'd hammered out the last details of my contract extension in September. If I was going to carry on, I told him, a few things needed to be changed and improved. There were personnel issues that we'd address by bringing in Vasi and Michael Mørkøv, but also things that needed to be tweaked and optimised on the technical side. I also – to be as frank now as I was with Vino – wanted and thought I deserved more money. Ultimately the success of the team and its future would be resting on my shoulders, with my story clearly one of the most intriguing narratives of the coming cycling season. There were riders in the team paid significantly more than me. We finally settled on a price and, albeit without too much fanfare, could finally confirm that I'd re-signed for 2024 in the first week of October.

The following week I flew to Turkey and did exactly as Vino said: no heroics, no busting a gut to win a stage or even sprint. Just work for the team, spend time on the front of the peloton, position our climbers and treat the race as the first step towards the Tour in July. It turned into the perfect week, with our star climber, Alexey Lutsenko, winning a stage and the overall.

Next stop was the presentation of the 2024 Tour de France route in Paris. This was another important waypoint on my journey to the following July. I was nervous – so much so that I'd already tried to tap up my contacts at A.S.O. to find out what I could expect. 'Don't worry … there'll be a fair few sprints,' was the message. The race was going to start in Italy for the first time ever. Not only that but it was starting in my 'adopted' home region, Tuscany, in the city where I'd first fallen in love with Italy, Florence. A.S.O. had in fact unveiled the first four stages ahead of the full route presentation. They consisted of one extremely hilly one heading east to the Adriatic coast, a similar one heading back, a relatively flat stage and probably a sprint in Turin (finally!) and then the return to France via one of the highest, hardest climbs in the Alps, the Col du Galibier.

Now, in the Palais des Congrès in Paris, I waited to discover what would come next ... and gulped when the profiles for the remaining 16 stages flashed across the giant screen behind where Christian Prudhomme stood on the stage. I'd never seen such a difficult Tour route, or one so clearly, if not deliberately, set up to make the sprinters' lives difficult. I glanced over my shoulder and caught the eye of my friend in the Tour organisation who had assured me that it'd be fine, that I was really making a good decision by giving it one last shot. He was laughing.

I'd seen and ridden brutal Tour routes before, but none where the difficulty and position of the climbs presented such a challenge to my particular skillset and, well, limitations. After stage four, it was true, came a run of flatter stages where I'd get several opportunities. In theory I could strike early, get the record and no one would care if I then quit or even got eliminated in the mountains packed into the second half of the race. But, in contrast to the dominant sprinter of the era before mine, Mario Cipollini, I'd never gone into the Tour with the intention or even vague idea that I wouldn't finish, even if that was always a possibility. The only exception had been the two years when I'd also been targeting track success at the Olympics. The Tour had been created as an endurance event, a challenge – a journey to be completed as much if not more than a race. I'd always remembered and tried to honour that. The biggest win for the majority of riders who ever race the Tour is reaching Paris, or, in 2024, Nice, given that's where we'd be finishing.

Now I looked again at the map, speechless, and allowed the consequences of the decision I'd taken a few weeks earlier to sink in. At this precise moment, that decision felt like a bad one. Nevertheless, I'd made a promise to my family, my team and myself. All in. Last time. Fuck, I'd tattooed a red triangle on my forearm just to remind me that this was it, the finishing straight, that I just had to keep moving forward and over the line.

So that's what I would do.

In training, this was also the mantra: keep moving, never stop … not even for the week or ten days off the bike that most riders give themselves in October or November. A few years earlier I'd ridden in the same Omega Pharma–QuickStep team as another leading sprinter of the generation that preceded mine, Alessandro Petacchi, and he'd given me that advice: as the years pass, the harder it becomes to lose weight and get back up to speed after a winter break … so don't give yourself a break. I'd also learned over the years that a solid, consistent winter was the best insurance policy against whatever imponderables training and racing might throw your way in the crucial weeks of summer and spring. A deep, wide base carefully constructed over the winter was one that could absorb stress and fatigue and react predictably. In my early years, relatively speaking, I'd been able to 'wing it' and got away with a fast-track preparation for the Tour in the last six or eight weeks; my age would have made the same approach at best risky, at worst impossible now. The mental stress of playing catch-up, being behind the curve, also drains your mental resources. My age and the fact that, because of it, my body simply didn't respond to training as quickly or efficiently as a younger rider's, already put me at a natural disadvantage that had to be, if not cancelled out, then at least not compounded. Again, I'd vowed to go all in … so that's what I'd do.

· · ·

Throughout the autumn and winter, my body felt good; I was motivated and clocking up long rides on the road, plus sometimes as many as six hours on my indoor trainer. At our first training camp in Spain, there was also a noticeable difference from the previous year, with Vasi now pulling the strings. No longer did the group rides consist of, basically, just races up climbs: there was structure, purpose, some science to what we were doing. I felt fit, happy … but also emotionally connected to the team and what was now our common goal in a way I hadn't been the previous year. In 2023 I'd arrived like a last-minute bargain Vino had found a few minutes before the shops closed on Christmas Eve and stuffed into a stocking. I'd never considered riding for Astana before, had certainly never envisaged finishing my career there, and throughout the season a certain sense of displacement or not really knowing what or who I was representing had remained. I felt, to put it bluntly, a bit like a mercenary, a soldier of fortune.

After Turkey, I'd had one last, big trip on my schedule for the autumn. Vino was turning 50 and wanted me to come with him to Kazakhstan to celebrate. He'd show me the country, the culture, the team's roots, he said. I was curious, intrigued, but, also, ultimately, it was my boss inviting me to a landmark birthday: I couldn't really opt out.

I went with no expectations apart from what I'd gleaned from conversations with Vino and my Kazakh team-mates over the previous few months. And, to be frank, in those, there was sometimes more emphasis on what Kazakhstan definitely was not than what it actually was. Let's just say that the name 'Borat' came up a lot. And that the comedian who invented that character is not exactly popular with most Kazakhs, and certainly wasn't with my team-mates. I'd try to tell them that the joke was actually on us ignorant Westerners, that it was our clueless stereotypes that were being lampooned, but they didn't buy it.

What I realised more or less as soon as I stepped off the plane was that this was a land that defied any attempt to generalise. Culturally, geographically and even historically, it seemed to me to sit at the intersection of completely different worlds. You could see the hyper-modern and pre-industrial juxtaposed on the same street, literally next door.

Asian and European. Remnants of the Soviet Union alongside still living, breathing legacies of the Mongol Empire. Roads flanked by tiny shacks and enormous five-star hotels, shared by horses and glistening new Mercedes. A Salvador Dalí painting writ large, brought to life in the world's biggest landlocked country.

For the next few days it was as though I was taking in sights, sounds and smells that my brain didn't have the codes to process. I was mesmerised, as I had been on my first trips to the Far East years earlier, when everything seemed different from what I knew. The first night was Vino's birthday. A 'small do', I'd been told – 'only' around 300 people at a fancy golf club just outside Almaty, the old capital. Dinner: course after course of delicious Kazakh delicacies – starter, two mains, dessert … then half an hour's break, followed by more mains, more soups, meats, and the same thing all over again. Just a whole night, hours and hours of eating. And speeches: every single person in the room, all 300-odd of us, each standing up to give our own little monologue, the whole thing lasting several hours, with every word patiently translated for me by one of Vino's friends.

Then the vodka, another new world in itself that I discovered that night. Of course it wasn't just a drink but also a whole ritual, which I violated immediately, heinously, by offering to pour a glass for the lady sat next to me, not realising that at these occasions the Kazakhs believe in strict segregation: champagne for women and vodka for men.

I could tell immediately from her horrified expression that I'd committed some sort of heresy … Fortunately, one of my fellow guests had soon given me a crash course, including in tasting. It was like a sort of ancient form of yoga: take some food, smell it, sip of vodka, then glass down, eat the food and savour the taste. Rinse and repeat. All night. Miraculously, I stayed at the same level of light, pleasant tipsiness the whole time, and woke the next morning with a perfectly clear head. I've never been a big consumer and certainly wouldn't glorify drinking now … but it was, shall we say, illuminating.

The night melted into the next day and another full programme of, ahem, cultural events. First, a mass-participation ride with 2,000-odd fans, followed by what Vino had promised would be a short warm-down in a much smaller group to a 'nice lunch spot'. He didn't mention that the 30-kilometre 'encore' was straight up a mountain almost to the Kyrgyzstan border. Or that, after lunch, we'd spend the afternoon in a sauna in the woods, butt-naked except for the traditional, tea-cosy-like felt hats perched on our heads.

It was an unusual starting point for any journey, and certainly what I hoped would be the last push to both the summit and final destination for my career as a rider in a few months' time. Equally, when I left Kazakhstan after a few days and certainly in the subsequent months, with hindsight, I'd come to see how the trip had given me something I'd lacked the previous year. I wasn't about to become a global ambassador for the Great Nation of Kazakhstan, not in any more formal capacity than wearing the Astana jersey at races, but I at least now felt an emotional connectedness that had been missing the previous year. People could think what they liked about Vino and why there was even a Kazakh team in the WorldTour in the first place – but I'd seen with my own eyes how proud he and they made the kind of ordinary folk I met in Almaty. I wasn't some sort of cycling missionary, and mine wasn't some noble humanitarian mission, but it did have some meaning beyond my own personal ambition and even beyond my family and what they wanted for me. Equally, my emotional connections and my environment had always impacted my performance, be it for good at QuickStep in 2021 or bad at Dimension Data in 2018 and 2019 in particular. This year, my last year, would be no different.

• • •

Kazakhstan wouldn't be the only 'exotic' journey of the close season. Vasi had studied the Tour route and reached broadly the same conclusion as me: our efforts over the next few months would have to be focused on my climbing, and that meant spending significant chunks of time at altitude. Vasi also said he had a brilliant idea: instead of following the hordes of GC riders holing up 2,000 metres above sea level on Tenerife or Gran Canaria … we would go to Colombia. We'd spend a couple of weeks training on the high plateau just outside Medellín, then go ever higher into the mountains surrounding Boyacá, then round off the trip by racing in Tour Colombia. The basic principle of altitude training is that the body learns to function with less oxygen available in the air. Riding at sea level then seems 'easy' – or at least the heart and lungs suddenly have a buffer zone, beyond their previous limit. The science that's emerged in recent years also suggests that going to altitude once, months before a big objective, makes it easier to re-stimulate the body in the same way if you return later, closer to the goal.

I'd had very limited and, to be frank, inconclusive experience with altitude camps, but Vasi was adamant and I trusted him. And so off we went, in early January, to another country I'd never visited, this time on the opposite side of the world, and with half a dozen team-mates. Once again, I was in for a huge culture shock. Mainly, I'd never been anywhere so completely besotted with cyclists and cycling. Before going I'd seen pictures and heard stories about riders needing police escorts on their training rides; I'd assumed, mistakenly, that this was because pro cyclists had occasionally been targeted by gangs; only now, when we trained with our own 'protection', organised by Vasi, did I realise that this was necessary just to keep fans on bikes or hanging out of car windows, tooting their horns and shouting our names, at a safe distance.

Rarely do you feel 'good' at altitude – particularly in the first few days – and this was no different. As the days went by, though, I could also feel myself getting stronger – and our group becoming more connected off the bike, and more in sync when we did sprint efforts on the bike. The days were long and, in the rarefied air, witheringly hot. Evenings were spent playing UNO or, our new obsession, a Russian card game introduced to me a few months earlier by Gleb, Durak. On training rides we also found or invented challenges to keep ourselves amused. For example, trying, with a full lead-out train, to break the 80-kilometre per hour barrier. When, after several attempts, we finally achieved that milestone, we celebrated as though we'd won a race. Any cars or bystanders who saw us jumping up and down, hollering and high-fiving at the side of a random road deep in the Andes, must have wondered what the fuck was going on.

As it turned out, it wouldn't be the only 'victory' of the trip. Stage four of Tour Colombia took us to Zipaquirá, the hometown of the 2019 Tour de France winner, Egan Bernal, 2,600 metres above sea level in the highlands to the north of Bogotá. After a nasty climb early on the stage, the main peloton split in half, with me in the second group and seemingly doomed … until Lutsenko dropped back from the front of the race to rescue and drag my whole group back. Then, on the run-in, we gathered ourselves and proceeded to deliver a sprinting clinic. It was my second win for Astana, my first since the last stage of the Giro the previous year. Three days later, the crowds for the final stage of this race, in Bogotá, were like nothing I'd ever seen, maybe not even in mountain stages at the Tour de France. That day was too hilly for me but we were going home with our ears ringing, our bodies tired but our faith renewed.

All those kilometres at altitude would be like money in the bank, gaining interest until the Tour. At least that was the idea, Vasi's idea. Unfortunately, it's never quite that simple where the human body is concerned ... and training for a professional cyclist is often more like pouring your hard-earned salary into an index fund: generally your fitness will trend upwards, but you're never immune from unforeseen downturns or, occasionally, a complete market crash. My Epstein–Barr virus had been my Great Recession in the years from 2017 to 2019. Sometimes the market – or in our case the body – follows its own stubborn logic. As I was about to learn once again.

After Colombia, the next race on my programme was the UAE Tour, starting just a week later. This was one of the more important stage races of the season, with a strong field. For most riders the first week or two after altitude training can be a challenge as the body goes into repair mode. I expected to feel sluggish, so there was no particular concern when I – and we as a team – struggled through the first few days. Stage six in Abu Dhabi would offer another chance, the last sprint of the race. I wasn't aware of feeling anxious or stressed. But as I lay in bed that morning, I noticed an odd sensation on the right side of my chest – a strange pulsing just beneath my armpit and across my ribcage. It was alarming enough for me to tell Mørkøv, who was lying in the single bed next to me. He promptly put down his phone and turned to face me. I pointed to the spot on my upper torso.

We could both now see the pulsing just under the skin.

'Fuck, you'd better get the doctor,' Mørky said.

The doc wasn't able to find or diagnose anything, but couldn't be sure. He prescribed a premature end to my race and for me to spend the next two days hooked up to an ECG. We wouldn't put out any statement about tests or any kind of scare, and instead just say that I had a 'small fever'. After the two days, in any case, the doctor reported that the ECG looked completely normal and my heart seemed fine. What exactly had happened that morning would remain a mystery.

Relieved and somewhat reassured, after another short stop to see the family, I headed to Italy for Tirreno–Adriatico. Same drill, same thought process: tough race, no pressure to win – full focus on the Tour de France. Easy to say, but a bit harder to fully, calmly assimilate when you're minutes off the back in each of the first four stages. And even harder when, on stage five, you finish outside the time limit and are eliminated from the race. That day it was the time cut itself that didn't make sense, more than my lack of form, but try convincing journalists or armchair experts on social media of that. I was well aware of the narrative that was already being woven: that Cavendish had made the classic, cardinal mistake of doing one year too many; that he was out of shape and out of sorts; that he'd get his backside handed to him at the Tour – if he even made it to the start line. Naturally I'd heard it all before. Which didn't mean that it didn't irritate and exasperate me.

Of course criticism is also most painful when it holds a grain of truth. And not even I could dispute that, post-Colombia, my Tour preparation had hit some turbulence. After getting time cut from Tirreno and failing to finish the Milano–Torino one-day race, I went home to the UK and continued to feel listless and empty. We were now over a month downstream of the altitude camp – so that could still be the reason. I tried to explain to Peta and to Vasi but would end up using vague terms for hard-to-define symptoms, confusing all of us. Our initial assumption was that I'd got some sort of virus, or maybe Covid. I got my blood tested and, after one first, anxious glance at the results, thought we had an answer: Epstein–Barr again. My markers were low. Fuck. That was it. Game over. Career over.

Only, no, the doctors – and by now I had a few of them trying to figure it out – said that wasn't it. Some blood markers were off, but it wasn't Epstein–Barr. Huge relief … but still no confident diagnosis or for that matter prognosis I could cling to, either. When I wasn't training or busy with the kids, one activity now monopolised my time: googling symptoms, trying to work out what the fuck was wrong. And, of course, as anyone who's fallen into the same spiral knows, scaring myself with worse-case scenarios.

Next on the agenda was a training camp in Greece, like the ones that had got me ready for the 2021 and 2023 Tours.

We'd planned everything months earlier: the first week of the camp would be a holiday with the family, or at least active rest, with minimal training. But now of course I couldn't afford that luxury; instead Vasi rode on his scooter every morning from his house in central Athens and we spent whole days together, slogging down the coast road or up climbs. At least I was getting evenings with Peta and the kids … not that I could particularly relax. Suddenly another problem, or symptom, had appeared – another mysterious ailment. A sort of stabbing in my side – where I thought my liver or kidneys were – that could last a few minutes or longer than half an hour. Earlier in my career I'd had issues with acid reflux when I was stressed before races, but this was nothing like that. Again, I told Peta and Vasi, but also sought reassurance in the worst possible place: Google. And of course I found the opposite – a multitude of theories and doomsday diagnoses, from gallstones to terminal pancreatic cancer.

Unfortunately or fortunately, it is the destiny of the pro athlete to become hyper-sensitive to everything happening in their body – practically every cellular process. Our bodies are our factory, our business, our family's livelihood, and so it stands to reason that any slight tingle or twinge can feel like a cause for alarm, and any pain an existential threat. Vasi and Peta knew this, of course, and also knew that if I was complaining about something feeling amiss, it was because something *was* amiss. And so Vasi ordered more tests and scans from clinics in Athens. Blood tests, an ultrasound.

I anxiously waited for the results, sure they would be the final nail in the coffin of my Tour hopes, only to be given what sounded like an emphatic verdict and diagnosis by the radiologist who had done my ultrasound.

He turned away from the screen on which my vital organs were displayed and muttered a few words of Greek to Vasi.

Vasi then turned to me.

'He says that you're suffering from ... stress. That's all. Just stress.'

Huge relief again. Sort of. I honestly hadn't been conscious of the tension building over several months. I knew that I was obsessed, totally consumed by the goal of being ready for the Tour – but I'd thought of that as a positive, not a negative. I was irritable, more inclined to nitpick or complain about equipment than usual, but I believed that I was just addressing genuine issues that needed to be fixed in time for the Tour. Later, Peta told me that in her opinion it wasn't so much that as me looking for something, anything to blame for my training not going the way that I'd hoped. Some days it might be saddle height, another it was a pain or discomfort somewhere in my body. If I could only fix that one thing, then we'd be in business, on course for the Tour. That was Peta's (probably accurate) diagnosis.

In any case, now I had confirmation, proof that I was fine. And so on we trained, now just me behind Vasi's scooter, Peta and the kids having gone home. The only family I had left with me for the last two weeks of the camp was Vasi's, my surrogate, Greek family. They'd met and adopted me years earlier, on my first trips in 2021. Vasi's son had even declared one day that I needed a Greek name, preferably one with a Peloponnese favour, like his own – Anastopoulos. Thus was born my plate-smashing, moussaka-guzzling alter-ego, Markos Cavendishopoulos.

Unfortunately, Markos Cavendishopoulos felt a little too at home in the last fortnight of the camp, as the wind howled every day, transporting me straight back to the Isle of Man. One day, Vasi had me riding uphill and right into the teeth of the headwind: the bike just wasn't moving forward, and I flipped. I ranted, 'This is fucking bullshit.' Simply parked up at the side of the road and told Vasi I wasn't finishing the effort. I only remember and mention it now because, the whole season, despite all the anxieties and niggles, I had finished every single session Vasi prescribed, executed every effort. Almost every ride I did, every climb, was the 'last' time I'd ever be on that road or mountain or doing those intervals in that order, and so everything became easier. For most of my career I'd hated training alone, grinding away for hours in silence; yes, the thinking time can be therapeutic, but it can also be destructive if you're prone, as I am, to unhelpful rumination. I'd never loved the process for its own sake – that idea of 'going monk', closing myself off from everything, eliminating distractions – all the stuff you hear GC riders evangelise about. I'd never relished or got a kick out of that – but this, in my last year, with only Vasi for company and one ultimate, metaphorical finish line to aim for, was as close as I'd ever got.

We flew to the Tour of Turkey. I rode that as I had the previous year's edition – not getting hung up on results, focusing only on building endurance. I should have won the first stage, anyway, but got stuck on the wrong wheel. No biggie – the focus was July. For that reason, the most significant takeaway from that week – as well as the eight stages and 1,000+ kilometres of racing – was something that hadn't worked and urgently needed correcting. My chain kept dropping off the chainrings. It was nothing new to us, but the severity of the problem varied from one wheel brand to another. Almost a decade earlier, my then team and I had got to the bottom of what had already caused me similar issues: whenever I stopped pedalling and started again, I created a jamming motion that caused the freehub in my wheels to yank and slightly loosen my chain. It was a movement that was unique to riders like me and my pedalling style – basically our short legs and unusually fast cadence – and, hence, produced a problem that only we encountered. The question was how we solved it before the Tour. It would take several weeks, hours of conversations, and, finally, the team's wheel sponsor, Vision, announcing they had found a fix. I'd get my new wheels, with a new, 'skip-proof' freehub in time for the Tour de Suisse ... and my chain would never jump again.

We were now in the home straight. Last tweaks were being made, last kinks ironed out. In most areas the work had begun months earlier. Once again, I knew that my age and basic physiology had stacked the odds against me, so I had to eke out every advantage, explore every possible hack that could make the difference. Some teams could throw money at every problem, whereas we'd have to be smart – which is why early in the year I'd called Alex Dowsett. A pro for over a decade, the winner of a Giro TT in 2013 and former hour record holder, Alex had retired from racing at the end of 2022. He was from Essex, not far from where Peta was born and where I'd spent most of the last decade. We'd often trained together when he was still racing … but now it was his expertise, rather than his company on long rides, that I wanted to tap into. Specifically, I knew Alex was one of the sharpest lateral-thinking minds around when it came to optimising aerodynamics. I didn't know exactly how he could help … but I knew he could. And I was right: soon we were in a wind tunnel at Silverstone, testing helmets, positions, shoe covers, clothing, exploring every possible way I could save just a few watts, gain a fraction of a second or a tyre-width in a sprint. There were plenty of aerodynamics gurus in cycling but they were engineers who spoke the language of engineers rather than bike racers. Alex was fluent in both. He was knowledgeable, professional and thought of every-thing. Case in point: ten minutes before our time in the wind tunnel was up, he said he had one more thing to try, and pulled two aerodynamic water bottles from his magic ruck-sack of tricks. After we'd run the numbers, it turned out they would save almost as many watts as other adjustments that had taken years of research, months of refinement and would cost thousands of pounds.

Finally, all the pieces seemed to be falling into place, and everyone was rallying around. Alex, who was phenomenal. My son Finn, whom I'd given a role as a sort of project manager for the custom skinsuit we were getting made at huge expense. The team's bike sponsors, Wilier Triestina, who'd initially winced when, on a visit to the factory in March, I'd suggested we forego one of their beautiful paintjobs on my Tour bike in favour of a splattered, spray-can effect, to save 150 grams. They'd not only agreed to that but had a brand-new climbing bike for me to try for the first time at the Tour de Suisse in June. Vasi, who'd broken down, simulated and planned out every stage of the Tour to the exact number of watts I needed to push on every metre of tarmac. Vino. My mental performance coach, David Spindler, who'd already said he'd fly to Greece for our last training sessions right before the Tour. Peta, as always.

They, we, were like an army assembling, my army, ready to go into battle for me for the very last time. The team, too, was shaping up. We went to the Tour of Hungary at the start of May and nailed the lead-out on stage two, Cees Bol and Mørkøv delivering me like I was riding in the back of a limousine. From Hungary, it was then time for the second and last big block of altitude training, 2,300 metres above sea level in the Sierra Nevada mountains of southern Spain.

Three weeks at the 'High Performance Centre' – basically boarding school for elite endurance athletes, Hogwarts for Olympic runners and Tour de France cyclists. The best riders in the world, shuffling half-asleep around the canteen with their trays, looking for the cornflakes, bumping into marathon world-record holders, knowing that 'class' starts in 20 minutes – not double maths but a double threshold session. You get the picture. It seemed like half of the peloton we'd meet again at the Tour de France in a few weeks' time was up there: Pogačar and UAE, Vingegaard and Visma, Remco Evenepoel and Soudal … You'd see their groups on the road and give them a wave or nod, but the groups sort of circled the mountains like prize wrestlers around a ring, suspiciously sizing each other up. We did long, hot days, descending 30 or so kilometres off the plateau towards Granada, training mainly in the valley and then climbing slowly back up towards base. Or, sometimes, getting into Vasi's team car and letting him drive us up the mountain. Vasi and I were under no illusion: surviving the mountains would be the biggest challenge of the Tour, but, equally, too much climbing could take the edge off my sprint. We were threading a needle, dancing between two extremes, trying to blend rocket fuel with marathon oil. Halfway through the Sierra Nevada camp I turned 39 – which only emphasised that I was also balancing on another knife edge: between a young man's body and middle age, the life of an athlete and my beckoning retirement.

Each night in the Sierra Nevada camp, before bedtime, our team's mental wellbeing coach, Piermarino Rosti, led us through yoga and breathwork exercises. I was pleasantly surprised to feel the benefits ... while also thinking, *This is all I need: more time to contemplate my own mortality.*

CHAPTER 10

In the build-up to the start of my final Tour de France there was a story about me, and the Italian city where the race was starting, Florence, that never got reported. It had nothing to do with me owning a house up the road in Quarrata or calling Tuscany 'my second home'. It wasn't about how much Italian I spoke or how many Vespas I owned or how I was occasionally partial to the Florentine 'delicacy' *lampredotto* – a sandwich filled with the slow-cooked 'fourth-belly' of a cow.

It was the story of a victory – in stage 13 of the 2009 Giro d'Italia. There was also a link with where the Tour would be rolling out on 29 June – on the same stretch of road, the Viale degli Olmi, where I'd won that day in Giro, 15 years earlier.

The whole truth about that day, though, very few people knew. I'd never gone out of my way to reveal it, because this was the single one of my 54 Grand Tour stage victories about which I felt a little sheepish, even a bit embarrassed.

The stage was starting to the west of Florence, at Lido di Camaiore on the Tyrrhenian coast. It was also probably going to be my last stage at the Giro. We, that is, Columbia–HTC, had won the opening-day TTT in Venice, I'd taken the pink jersey the following day, then two stage wins, and now I'd be leaving the race ahead of the final week to get ready for the Tour. Just as most of the top sprinters did every year. Nothing unusual, nothing scandalous. The fact that I was also moving apartments in the Giro's last week and had a removal van booked? Pure coincidence.

My routine every day at the Giro had been the same. Every morning, 20 minutes before the stage roll-out I'd go to the hospitality tent for a coffee and to catch up with other riders. They would all then leave when they heard a bell that was rung five minutes before the start, while I'd linger a bit longer; I loved the Italian *tifosi* and how much they'd taken me to their hearts, but some days getting stopped for autographs every couple of metres or just pawed and prodded put me in a bad mood before we'd even started rolling. Much better to let the crowd around hospitality disperse or get distracted by other riders, then rock up to the line, relatively undisturbed, with 30 seconds to go, or even as the peloton was leaving.

Which is exactly what I intended to do on this day, except the location of the hospitality tents was a bit unusual, at the end of a pier. And when I hopped on my bike and started rolling down the boardwalk, towards where the start was, I couldn't find the way out. I was trapped. I'd wanted to avoid the crowds, but now I looked around for someone to let me out or point me in the right direction – a steward, a fan, anyone – and suddenly there was just confusion. Chaos. *Un gran casino*, as the Italians say. One minute of getting nowhere. Two. I tried left. Then right. Fucking barriers on every side. Panic. Three minutes and counting. No fucking way through and no sign of a gap in any barrier. FUCK! Now, on the other side of the water, 50 metres away, I could see the team cars speeding out of town, the bikes on their roof racks spooling past over the fans' heads, and the ambulance that marks the end of the convoy …

FUCK.

Finally, I found a way out. Tried to radio my team car to tell them I was stranded. 'Valerio! Valerio!' – Valerio Piva was our directeur sportif. But he couldn't hear. Nothing. They were already out of range. Fuck. Fortunately, I knew the route: I'd trained on these roads. It was before the days of navigation systems on our computers but I could find my way. The problem was that the crowds, the locals, had now spilled into the roads all around the start. The route was choked with people. By the time I'd done two or three kilometres, stopping or slowing every few seconds to dodge a pedestrian, the panic and horror had crystallised into a cold certainty: there was no way I was getting back into the race.

The only thing I could think of was a … short-cut. The first part of the stage was a loop – so could I sneak back on after 50 kilometres? I was ashamed of myself for even thinking it. Of course I fucking couldn't. It was the Giro d'Italia, not the Dick Dastardly Grand Prix ... Nope, for now I just had to bury myself, ride the time trial of my life, and pray the race slowed down.

So bury myself I did. For the best part of 20 kilometres. Then, a miracle: a Rabobank team car parked at the side of the road. One of their directeurs must have needed a 'nature break', they'd stopped, the whole convoy had gone past ... and now they, like me, had to get back into the race. I did my first sprint of the day to get into their slipstream, then, after two or three kilometres, finally, I could just about make out the ambulance and, snaking into the distance ahead of it, the cavalcade of team cars.

Fuck. I could finally breathe. Or would have if my heart hadn't been thumping at 200 beats per minute. A few more minutes and I was moving through the line of the cars, all the way to the back of the peloton, when, in my still-traumatised, hyperventilating state, I stupidly tried to go up the inside of the other Rabobank car on a corner. Splat, down I came.

I was saved now by the fact that my team car could see me and radio my team-mates. And that Rabobank had the race leader, Denis Menchov. My team-mate, Kosta Siutsou, only had to tell Menchov that I'd crashed and he could order the whole bunch to slow and wait. Today it'd be different, but back then such was the unspoken 'rule'.

I finally got back into the peloton after 23 kilometres. Five hours later I was crossing the line with my arms aloft.

• • •

Whether this was some sort of good omen – or just a cool story that I'd never really shared – I wouldn't have been able to tell you before the 2024 Grand Départ and still wouldn't now. I was a guy whose past achievements dominated every conversation about me – and yet at the same time the past didn't matter. Put another way: all certain people wanted to talk about was the record, how many stages I'd already won, yet mainly, it seemed to me, in the context of what I wouldn't be able to do, the landmark I wouldn't reach over the coming three weeks.

I was too far in to get distracted by the noise. History was one predictor of the future but the present was more reliable and more important. After the Tour de Suisse I flew straight to Greece, where Vasi and I attacked our last ten days of prep. The engine had been built over the previous few months. Now was about fine-tuning. One key area that I could focus on in that final fortnight was heat adaptation. Awareness around this had grown enormously over the previous few seasons, to the extent that nearly every Tour rider had incorporated some kind of high-temperature protocol into their training. Some riders would even set up their turbo trainers in a sauna. The best and most reliable method, though, seemed to be simply riding in very hot weather. This made Greece in mid-June the ideal location.

Physically, Vasi declared me ready to go, ready to win. David Spindler confirmed that I was also mentally locked in. Immediately after sprint efforts, we'd do reaction tests on an iPad – reps for the legs, then for the neurons. Those too, said Spindler, showed that I was fully operational.

While I was in Greece, another unexpected morale boost arrived: the news that I would be knighted. It was made doubly gratifying by the timing, before the Tour. The King thought I was worthy of the honour with or without a thirty-fifth Tour stage.

And so to Florence we went. Into the madness of the Tour for the final time, with the usual cocktail of excitement and dread. Dread mainly because of the suffering I knew I'd have to endure. Often in cycling people use the words 'pain' and 'suffering' interchangeably, but for me there was an important and maybe crude distinction: pain was like being punched in the face, suffering was like having your fingernails very slowly removed. What scared me about the Tour was the latter: I knew that at some point on every one of the 21 stages I'd be deeply uncomfortable, and that almost every day there'd be some suffering. I dreaded it because the Tour had always been a different level from every other race on the calendar, but in the last few years the gulf had somehow become even wider. All you could do was try to prepare yourself mentally and physically, while knowing that, whatever you imagined or feared, you'd get there and on the first day it'd be even worse. My dress rehearsal had been the mountains of the Tour de Suisse in June. I'd gone there with the sole objective of hardening myself – more specifically hardening my mind – to that experience of suffering without knowing exactly when it would end, at the mercy of riders who could simply climb much faster than me. When I survived the mountains there, my confidence soared. But it didn't altogether erase the dread.

As for the excitement, well, I couldn't change that either – and naturally didn't want to. It was pretty simple: for me, racing the Tour was like being home. This was the race that I'd dreamed about as a kid, the race that had defined me. There was nothing else in the sport like it. Not even close. It was as though the Tour flipped some primal switch in me. Rewired my whole nervous system.

The race starting in Florence added to that sense of being exactly where I belonged. Everything was familiar, from the location for the team presentation in Piazzale Michelangelo on the hill overlooking the city to the roads through the Apennines above Quarrata where I took the team for our last training ride. The heat, too, with its stifling humidity – with which I was well acquainted. In our pre-race briefing on the bus before stage one we re-emphasised the importance of staying cool. I wasn't worried – it'd be the same for everyone. And I was perfectly prepared.

Or so we believed.

There are two 'starts' in every regular stage or professional road race: what the French call the *départ fictif*, literally the fictional departure, where the peloton starts rolling, usually out of a town or city where road furniture may cause hazards; then another, the *départ réel* or real departure, often a few kilometres away, when the race actually commences on the open road. The first stage of the Tour de France is different in that we usually get three: the beginning of the 'roll-out' to a scenic or significant landmark where we all stop and there's a small ceremony to declare the Tour officially open or under-way; the bit when we get going from there again; and, finally, the *départ réel* or kilometre zero, where the chaos is finally, officially unleashed.

This year, we'd do four kilometres then stop outside in the Piazza della Signoria, Florence's most famous square, for the official 'opening ceremony', then set off again towards kilometre zero.

Piazza della Signoria is probably most famous for Michelangelo's statue of David (it's a replica – the real one is a few blocks away in a gallery). On this day it was also blaz-ing like Dante's Inferno. The temperature edged 35 degrees. The formalities also dragged on – 15, maybe 20 minutes. By the time they were over and we finally clipped back into our pedals, I was cooking from the inside out.

I didn't know immediately that I was in trouble. In fact my legs felt good, despite the blistering pace at the front of the bunch. It was hot, savagely hot – and fast, unnecessarily fast – but I was ticking along just fine. Then we got to the first climb after nearly an hour and it started: first, me getting chopped like a steak tartare. Ever since the start of my career it's been the same – no one wants to be on a sprinter's back wheel on a climb because they think he, the sprinter, will lose the one in front and they'll have to make a big effort to come around. So instead they 'chop' the sprinter, cut and carve him up – do anything to get ahead. The same happens in the finales of sprint stages but in reverse, the sprinters trying to get ahead of the climbers. I try to counteract it by hugging one side of the road, so that at least they can only come at me from one side. But here the knives were out and, as much as I'd learned over the years that getting angry only cost more energy, I was getting literally very hot and increasingly bothered.

I could feel my heart starting to hammer under my ribcage. I'd never worn a heart-rate monitor in races because I didn't like the discomfort of the chest-strap – plus I didn't need a digital display to tell me what I could already feel. Here, that clear message was: you're finding this way too hard. Unfortunately, that intuitive feedback was overridden by what I could see on another device, my power meter. This told me that I'd pushed these watts in training so needn't slow down. That was my next big mistake.

This is one of the issues with the data-driven – in fact data-obsessed – cycling that I'd soon be leaving behind: the numbers suck you in, against your better judgement, even if you're a rider who's aware of that danger and has spent years attuning yourself to your body's subtle signals. Once upon a time, in the same situation, I'd have turned to Bernie Eisel, my old team-mate and mountain sherpa in these situations, and told him, bluntly, that I was fucked and we needed to back off. We'd have leaked time steadily on the climbs and eaten it back on the descents. Now I'd let the numbers gaslight me. And was suffocating, completely 'blowing up' as a result.

Two things brought me 'comfort': one, my team-mates – Mørkøv, Gazzoli, Ballerini, Bol, who had clustered around me, drenching me with water and stuffing my jersey with ice the moment my 'distress call' went out on the radio; two, the fact that I was too far gone, too sideways to really process the misery of what was happening. Had I been able to zoom out, see myself as the millions watching me implode on live TV were seeing me, I'd have been able to appreciate the horror of what was unfolding. Friends described it to me later – the unfolding tragedy of what they thought they were watching. The naked delusion of a man who had thought he could go to the Tour de France at age 39 and make history, only to be embarrassed and ultimately eliminated within a couple of hours. It would have been one of the saddest, most undignified endings imaginable.

I think that most riders in my position would have got off their bikes. My young Italian team-mate, Michele Gazzoli, did just that after three climbs and with around 90 kilometres to go. At that point we were around 15 minutes behind the front of the race. A few kilometres earlier I'd been telling him to slow down, barely holding his wheel. Then he started swinging – straining to stay with us. We'd both been vomiting, literally retching on the bike, which for me wasn't unusual. But soon Gazzoli hadn't done a turn for a minute or two, I looked back and saw him dropping back to the team car. A few seconds later we got the message in our earpieces: 'Guys, Gazzoli has stopped. Gazzoli has abandoned.'

I'll confess that I was a little … disappointed. I hadn't done a lot of races with Gazzoli but I'd liked the kid immediately. Admittedly, I may have been swayed slightly by him telling me in our first conversations that I'd been his childhood hero. He'd worn the same shoes as me, asked for the same sunglasses for Christmas, had my posters on his wall … He was also a bloody good rider who, I thought, deserved to take the last 'available' slot in our Tour team. That day on the Tour it looked to me as though we were both going through the same ordeal – that he, like me, had overheated and then imploded. Equally, though, this was the first stage of the Tour de France. Of course it was going to be hard. You had to block out the pain. Switch to manual override. Above all, just keep turning the pedals, use forward motion as an anaesthetic. Maybe the difference between us was just my experience of these situations, my 14 Tours to his none. I can't say. To be honest, since that day, we've never had the conversation about exactly what happened to him.

In those last 90 kilometres, anyway, my other team-mates did the work of two more men: Gazzoli and yours truly, who they simply dragged towards the finish line. I could have cried with gratitude. With their help, sheltering in their wheels, I was able to recover in the valleys and steel myself for the climbs. After the first hill, I never panicked.

Surviving, making the time cut, became nothing more than a maths problem requiring a methodical approach. Soon we were catching riders who had made the same mistake as me on that first climb, gone beyond their limit. They were now boomeranging back towards us, cross-eyed. Thankfully for us those same riders also now added some firepower on the flat, giving us an even bigger buffer. We'd finally cross the line 39 minutes after the stage winner, Romain Bardet, 10 minutes inside the time limit.

Over the previous few months Vasi and I had talked endlessly. About how I was going to win but mainly how I was going to survive. His thesis went more or less as follows: the deeper into the Tour the other sprinters rode, the worse they got, whereas my powers of recovery could become my biggest advantage. Basically, he'd tell me, with every stage we overcame, the more the game would be rigged against them and in my favour. By the same logic, he managed to turn the basic principle of endurance on its head, at least insofar as it applied to me: the further I went, the less fatigue I accumulated relative to my rivals. Stage one would be my hardest day; from there on it would all become incrementally easier.

The Greeks had given us Plato, Socrates, Aristotle and, now, Anastopoulos with his Theory of Endurance. What a journey we'd been on together over the previous four years since I'd met him at QuickStep. From the start I'd loved his lack of bullshit and his passion ... once I'd got past his loudness. My epiphany came when I stepped into the departures hall at Athens airport on my first trip to Greece in the spring of 2021. 'Fuck, now I get it,' I told him later that day. 'You're all loud. Italians cranked up to eleven.' From then on it became my shorthand gag whenever he or anyone else was being over-boisterous, a bit 'extra': 'Stop being so Greek …' Or just a roll of the eyes and a laconic, 'Yep, Greeks.' It was of course said in jest, with affection, and Vasi knew what he and his family meant to me after all those training camps over the years. We've covered the Markos Cavendishopoulos nickname, but new for this Tour was the launch of the unofficial, official 'Markos Cavendishopoulos Fan Club'. Vasi had made up T-shirts and distributed them to various friends and people I'd met over the years on my trips to Greece. They had all then sent me selfies in the days leading up to the Tour.

Most important was that Vasi's faith in me had never wavered. Not in 2021, not in 2023 when I wasn't even sure if I wanted to carry on, and not even when I looked to other people as though I was capitulating on stage one. Typically, in training, whenever he set me a challenge or series of efforts, and I'd hit his targets, he'd respond with faux indignance and a 'Fuck you!' I'd smile then we'd both collapse in giggles.

Now, in Rimini, there were no compliments disguised as insults, no celebrations or histrionics. Almost immediately, our thoughts turned to stage two. 'It'll be fine, just stick to the plan,' Vasi said, producing the numbers that he'd worked out months earlier – the exact watts I'd have to push on every one of the six classified climbs.

Sure enough, by comparison, and in accordance with Anastopoulos's Theory of Endurance, the next day I got through just fine. It was on to Turin – the first chance of this Tour to make history for the last time.

• • •

Over the course of the three weeks there'd be lots of opportunities or invitations to look back over my Tour de France career – all 18 years, 14 editions and 36,168 kilometres of it to that point – but in the main I tried not to dwell. In general, the early years and first Tours could seem like a lifetime ago. I'd been given my chance to ride for T-Mobile in 2007 basically because I'd written the directeurs sportif an email persuasively arguing that they pick me for a Tour starting for the first time in the UK. I ended up being somewhat out of my depth, but a lot of what I wrote in that email was nonetheless vindicated: about my presence bringing the sponsors publicity at a time when cycling was ready to explode in the UK, and about how even an 'unsuccessful' first experience of the Tour would stand me and us in good stead for future years.

The first sprint of that 2007 Tour had come in stage two in Canterbury – and I didn't see, let alone contest it. From the moment we'd rolled out of London, I was crackling with agitation and anxiety. Hearing me scream into my radio after a puncture, the Spanish rider Juan Antonio Flecha practically grabbed me and told me I needed to calm down. He was right, but I didn't have the experience or, at that point, the emotional control. I'd finish the stage in tears, having crashed with 25 kilometres to go.

Fast forward 18 years and one thing hadn't changed – the first sprint stage of the Tour is always the most chaotic, the most stressful and dangerous of the race. No hierarchy has yet been established, no pecking order among the sprinters' teams, and to their anarchy is added the turf war between GC riders and their domestiques. Later in the year, we'd have a riders' night out after the Saitama Criterium in Japan and, after a few drinks, I'd get into a heated debate about this with a rider who had recently finished on the podium of a Grand Tour. His argument, very broadly, was that sprinters had no right to kick off about GC riders crowding the front of the bunch in sprint stages because we did the same to them before climbs. It ended up getting pretty feisty and, given that we were in a public place – a restaurant – maybe even a little undignified. Admittedly not as undignified as him getting blind drunk and collapsing on one of the sport's leading decision-makers in a lift at 6am the following morning.

In any case, right or wrong, I knew the drill – and sure enough the stampede began noticeably earlier than in 'usual' Tour stages. This wasn't the only stress: I also punctured twice. For a few years now it had become fairly common practice for teams to use super-thin, super-fast time-trial tyres in 'normal' stages. They might only 'last' 200 or 300 kilometres, one day at the Tour, but their lower rolling resistance offered a significant advantage. Tadej Pogačar apparently used them on every stage, and now we were on sprint days, too. Only we'd evidently received a bad batch, because that day our tyres were popping like bubble wrap after only 60 or 70 kilometres. The rubber on the tyre walls was simply wearing through, disintegrating.

This wasn't the first issue we'd had with equipment since arriving in Italy. The supposedly supersonic, eye-wateringly expensive tailored skinsuit I'd tested with Alex Dowsett and ordered months earlier had turned into a nightmare. One version had come back with a zip in the wrong place, then they'd fixed that but somehow turned the team's signature turquoise colour a spearmint green. Peta hadn't intended to come to Florence but ended up having to jump on a plane two days before the race to deliver the begrudgingly altered final version. An attempt to get our team helmet supplier to add a couple of minor aerodynamic enhancements had proved similarly frustrating. Having at first agreed, they matter-of-factly informed us three days before the race that it simply hadn't been possible and that I'd just have to make do. Meanwhile, without my blessing, they'd already launched and put on sale a Mark Cavendish 'signature' edition.

The punctures had at least come early enough for us to regroup. With three kilometres to go we were well set, nestling nicely about 20 wheels back. Then it came: that familiar noise of metal on metal, flesh on metal, then a percussion section of all three together: metal, flesh and tarmac. Followed by a medley of groans and moans. I was safely behind the falling bodies, but also stuck behind them. I watched the lucky ones on the other side of the chaos riding away to contest the sprint finish like a stranded passenger left on the dock, watching their ship sail over the horizon.

A bitter pill was sugared somewhat when I rolled over the line to discover that Biniam Girmay was the stage winner. This made it a huge moment for the Tour de France. Biniam's was the first ever victory in the race for a Black African rider. Immediately, this felt seismic. Besides its symbolism, what it would mean for a whole continent that had been shamefully denied opportunities for as long as bike racing had existed in its parochial western European bubble, it was also a victory for one of the most popular riders in the peloton. 'Legend' was, I think, the word I used in interviews that night, and I meant it in more ways than one.

I didn't profess to be an expert on the difficulties African cyclists had encountered and overcome but my time at Dimension Data, the first and to date only African top-tier team to exist, had given me some insight. I'd had numerous Eritrean team-mates, in particular. They'd taught me about how colonisation by the Italians in the late nineteenth and twentieth centuries had left a curious legacy – an enduring, country-wide passion for bike racing. They'd also described their struggles to get adequate equipment when they were growing up, or the recurring nightmare of applying for visas when they wanted to race in Europe later. Equally, those who had somehow made it then had to negotiate their way around or through another, seemingly opposite conundrum: receiving too much adulation, maybe excessive privilege and status. From the little I knew or had seen of Biniam's route, he'd been 'lucky' in the sense that just getting to Europe hadn't been his El Dorado. He'd landed in a small French team that went bust, and continued to fight and scrap for his dream: not just making it to sport's biggest races but also being successful, winning on the biggest stage. Later, after he'd won two more stages of the Tour and the even more historic prize of the green jersey, I asked him whether he'd soon be heading home to celebrate and he admitted he was slightly terrified of the hysteria he'd unleashed. Someone had already turned up unannounced at his house and repainted the whole thing green. Bini was grateful for the support, proud of his roots and also keen to give back … but he was also, mainly, focused on winning more of the sport's biggest races.

For me of course, one more would have done … and an opportunity had already slipped by. I'd also have to wait for the next chance, as the Tour was now heading into France via the Alps. The Col du Galibier loomed – a big, alpine bastard of a climb, one of the highest and toughest in the range. The finish line was on the other side of the summit in Valloire. Get past this stage and we'd finally be on flatter terrain for the rest of the first week, but the Galibier stood guard like a giant, scowling nightclub bouncer blocking my path to the dancefloor.

The hatchet-face doorman must have woken that day in a good mood – or at least I was able to sweet-talk him and breeze past. We stuck to our plan, rode our pace on the first two climbs of the day. Then, when the road turned right and steepened, nine kilometres from the summit of the Galibier, we – my team-mates and I – clicked into energy-saving mode. Sometimes I had to smile, watching other sprinters hammering up mountains ahead of us. The time limit was no issue: we had a 10- or 12-minute cushion. So why weren't they saving their watts for the sprint the following day? The answer of course was 'ego' – something that I'd learned to set aside years earlier in the mountains. I'd long since accepted that God hadn't designed me to go uphill. Or, if he did, his project manager needed replacing. I had a single talent and every other resource needed to be harnessed and utilised to showcase that prize pony's single trick. In a sport that had become obsessed with one metric – the ratio of watts to body weight in kilograms, ergo how fast you went uphill – I was concerned with a different, some might say more primitive equation: watts to wins.

Victory on this day meant surviving the Galibier, and I'd done that. For the second day in a row I was also delighted to discover the name of the actual stage winner. Tadej Pogačar had dropped Jonas Vingegaard on the last ramps of the Galibier then soloed to the finish and also taken the yellow jersey.

My whole family adored Pogačar. For Casper, who at age two was making us turn off *Peppa Pig* and switch on midweek mountain stages in the Tour of the Basque Country, Tadej was nothing short of a god. I was also in awe of him, as much for how he conducted himself off the bike as what he could do on it. I experienced some of what he does now – the constant demands on your time, the literal and figurative prodding, the scrutiny. Your defeats being a bigger story than your victories. The entitlement of the people creating and perpetuating those narratives. But I didn't have the same emotional firewall as him. He was configured for coolness in a way that defied my understanding. Nice to everyone in the bunch, respectful, a good loser on the rare occasions when he didn't crush everyone. Many of the same things applied to his 'eternal' rival, Jonas Vingegaard, incidentally. I'd first come across him in 2021 when he was still unknown outside of Denmark and I was just starting to see the first rays of light after four years of gloom at a small Italian race, the Settimana Coppi e Bartali. He went on to win that race and, then, a few months later, finish second in the Tour behind Tadej. Also a lovely guy and phenomenal athlete … who just had the misfortune to be competing against an even more prodigious talent, in my opinion.

The only thing that frustrated me about Tadej was that he should have been more famous. The kid was a showman, a gentleman, spoke perfect English, and yet his achievements barely seemed to resonate beyond cycling's echo chamber. He should have been Tom Brady, Michael Jordan … and yet cycling hadn't been able to give him the same platform. That didn't reflect well on the sport, its past or its future. Equally, I'd been hearing the same discordant, frankly tedious conversations about business models, new revenue streams and how cycling could and should market itself more effectively for 20 years. I was as tired of them as I was of climbing mountains. They were topics for later. Maybe for my retirement.

For now, that dancefloor I'd been eyeing on the other side of the Alps was calling my name. It was time to see if the old dude in button-down shirt and dress shoes could still throw a few shapes.

CHAPTER 11

I t was a day like any other on the Tour de France, a day like every one of the 215 I'd done to that date at the greatest bike race in the world. I slowly opened then rubbed my eyes and took a moment to process what I could see through the half-light.

Valloire. Same place we finished yesterday. Fuck. Got it. Little ski chalet. Nice people. Galibier yesterday, sprint stage today. OK.

Mørky? Still asleep.

Time? 8.30. Nearly five hours until the start. Sound.

So it had gone, with just hotel-room interiors and the bodies in the twin beds next to me changing for nearly two decades. I forced my eyelids a little further apart and surveyed a little more of the, ahem, luxury in which we'd spent the last few hours. Above my head, the underside of a top bunk that neither of us had used; across the room, another bunk bed with my suitcase open on the lower deck. Three or four carefully stacked towers of Mørky's clothing peeking over the brow of his open case on the floor. Two race numbers stuck side by side to the wooden slats of one of the beds.

On a shelf next to my bed, the last thing I could remember looking at last night: the Tour de France roadbook, once the race 'Bible' but increasingly something that only riders of my generation seemed to use – a sort of dinosaur's digest for the soon-to-be has-beens.

Usually now it was purely revision. We knew and had studied every finish, and Mark Renshaw had driven and videoed many of them. Still, there was no such thing as too much information, and so I messaged my old mate Pete Kennaugh, who was working for ITV and would already be at the finish. Would he mind taking a bike out, riding the last couple of kilometres and filming it for me? Google Street View, satellite pictures and even the roadbook were helpful, but you never knew from looking at them how the barriers would be set up, exactly how the wind was blowing through the trees.

A minute or two later Pete had given me a blue tick and 'no problem'.

Sound. Cool. That's that. Time now: 9am. Mørky's stirring. Shower. Check messages. Tell Peta and the kids good morning, love them. Take picture of this shoebox we've just slept in and send to a mate who's taunting me with photos of some posh dinner on the other side of the world. Throw on clothes. Go downstairs. Breakfast.

I can remember feeling nervous. There was no particular reason why, or not one that I could pinpoint. It was also not a feeling that I wanted to fight. Excitement and anxiety are the same emotion with the same by-product: adrenaline. You don't fight that; you feel it, soak it up, turn it into fuel.

Breakfast. Again, same for years: big bowl of Special K, couple of coffees. Always espresso. Then two pancakes on the bus an hour and a half before the start, just to top up my glycogen. Learned that from the nutritionist at QuickStep a few years ago. Look around the breakfast room and for once don't see other riders with their digital scales, measuring out and weighing their food. Another 'marginal gain' … but FUCK that. What's the difference between two slices of bread? One gram? Five grams at most? Nah, tried that once. Got me nowhere. Also a bit late to start again now. Two weeks to go …

Back upstairs. Pack.

Before I left for every Tour, Peta slipped a book into my luggage – a little photo album that she'd made, different every time, with photos of the kids. Every day I'd pull it out before I closed my case and it'd make me smile. There was also a video on my phone that melted my heart. In it, Astrid, who was about to turn two, was doing ballet – ten or so seconds of her twirling around in a tutu, waving a wand, beaming, making her own sound effects: 'Bibidee bobbidee boo … Bibidee bobbidee boo …' Before the Tour, in Greece, as part of our mental preparation, David Spindler had asked me what filled me with joy. I'd told him about the video, and then he'd explained how we could use it. I'm paraphrasing, no doubt oversimplifying, but thinking about things that brought me joy could apparently release chemicals, neurotransmitters, that dulled pain or slowed fatigue and enhanced performance. This chimed with what I'd heard from other riders about taking anti-depressants – that boosting the same neurotransmitters had also helped on the bike. I hadn't wanted to take them but I didn't mind someone reminding me of Astrid doing ballet.

Onto the bus and to my usual seat, in the middle of the rows. Everyone files in, wheels roll. Journey time: 45 minutes, maybe an hour to the start, down the Col du Télégraphe to Saint-Jean-de-Maurienne. OK. Sound. Renshaw gets up from his seat next to our driver and walks down the gangway, roadbook under his arm. Sits down. Committee meeting: Renshaw, Mørky, Cees and me. Same as every day. Agenda: last thoughts on the finish, the video Pete Kennaugh's sent, what Renshaw's going to tell the other lads in the briefing in a few minutes ... For now we leave the others be. Ballerini on his Nintendo Switch. The two Kazakhs, Lutsenko and Yevgeniy Fedorov, also hunched over iPads on either side of the aisle, peppering each other with virtual bullets on some shoot-'em-up video game, loudly taunting each other in Russian, then erupting with laughter. Harold Tejada, our little Colombian climber, in the row opposite me, silent and serene with his headphones on ... because, well, when was Harold not serene?

That day Harold would be key. The stage had been earmarked as one for us, a 'sprinters' stage', but that didn't mean it was completely or even remotely flat. The profile showed a 12-kilometre climb after 85 kilometres, then 3 kilometres uphill with 35 kilometres to go. Harold's job would be to lead us into the second of those two hills, where the road was narrow and the peloton would stretch into a long line. Any sprinter starting the climb more than 20 or 30 positions back would invariably lose ground and soon be in danger of losing touch altogether. But if Harold could get us to and keep us at the front for the first kilometre, he could then also set a pace that was right in 'our' sweet spot: too fast for anyone to attack, slow enough not to put me in trouble.

All of this, of course, was purely theoretical. Maybe wishful thinking. Bike races were harder to predict and certainly harder to control than earlier in my career. Logic might suggest that a team wouldn't go 'all in' on a climb to try to drop me because, in doing so, they'd also nuke their own domestiques. But bike racing nowadays often didn't obey logic. Also, course designers and particularly the Tour's, Thierry Gouvenou, now went out of their way to encourage exactly that type of move in the last hour of stages. The route of this stage exemplified that perfectly: the race was turning off a road just to go up a hill, then coming back onto the same road and carrying on towards the finish.

Bus parks. Get changed for sign on. Stick on race number. For the sprint stage two days ago I didn't wear the fancy, platinum-price skinsuit. There's a crash, like always in the first sprint stage, it gets shredded and that's thousands of pounds and hours of planning you've wasted … Today I'll wear it – fuck it – but I'm not putting it on until after sign-on. Don't want anyone seeing it. Photographing it. Don't want journalists or other riders asking about it.

I said that modern racing didn't obey logic but neither did my brain. Not wearing the special skinsuit to sign-on or putting the aero bottles on my bike really had nothing to do with getting spotted, another team or rival noticing and … well, I don't even know what they'd do with that information an hour before the start. It wasn't that simple. Clearly this was about me and the voice in my head. A desire to somehow fly under the radar, stay in stealth mode, maybe avoid putting extra pressure on myself. To be an underdog. Perhaps not admit to myself until the very last second that this was a big day, possibly *the* day. A sheepishness maybe grounded in years of feeling as though I didn't have the room or the right to fail, even to come second; or having learned that being attributed with potential was much easier (and in a lot of cases more lucrative) than defending a reputation or empire constructed over the duration of a career.

I didn't try to psychoanalyse it but deep down I recognised my instinct to hide from, deflect and resent the pressure. Maybe actually it was very simple: I expected so much from myself that any additional, unnecessary pressure from the outside made me bristle. An innocuous comment from another rider – 'Ooh, Cav, aero-bottles today, I see …' – could feel to me like added weight.

Peta and the kids waited outside the bus for Renshaw to finish the briefing. He emphasised two points we'd gone over half an hour earlier with the 'committee': that until the last kilometre I'd like to follow Cees, who's 6'4", so taller than Mørky, and would give me better shelter when the road was exposed; and the inside line I wanted to take in the last 500 metres as the road curved to the right – essentially going in a straight line across the apex of the bend and finishing on the left side of the road. 'OK, 20 minutes to the start,' were Renshaw's last words. There was no great rousing speech – no Al Pacino in *Any Given Sunday* moment, not even any overexuberance from Vasi. The atmosphere was calm, businesslike. A mood like any other day, except for the light flutter in my stomach, the whisper of anxiety through my thoughts and under my skin.

Last prep. Food. Everything in pockets because I can't trust the feedzones. Or, rather, I can't trust the other riders in feedzones. How is it that some of these kids have never learned to take a bottle? Who taught them when they were juniors …? Anyway, whatever, not risking it. Stage length today: nearly 180 kilometres so that's … eight feeds, eight times about 30 grams of carbs. Boom. Easy. Fill the pockets. Shoes on. Ready. We move.

Even with Peta and the kids I was quiet. Quieter than usual. We sat outside the bus for a few minutes on a grass verge. The kids ate Haribo and generally whirred around our heads causing chaos and noise. Casper, my six-year-old mini-me, our tearaway, who was probably thinking about who would lead out Philipsen, or whether Pogačar might try something on one of the climbs. Frey, who's not really interested but gets dragged along, at least gets to see his dad for a few minutes, just gets on with it, never complains … Delilah, 12, our sassy tribe leader. Finn, our eldest, who was at the finish. Peta had driven them 200-odd kilometres just for these few minutes together, and now she'd have to drive 200 more.

I said my goodbyes, gave them all a kiss and rode towards the start. Stopped to sign a couple of autographs, pose for selfies. Then onto the line and, a few minutes later, out we rolled. The Maurienne valley serves as base camp for some of the most infamous climbs in cycling. The Galibier, which we'd done the day before, but also the Col de la Madeleine and the Glandon. Today, thankfully, they were just names on road signs that flashed past my eyes rather than instruments of torture. Soon the sheer, glowering mountainsides to our left and right were slanting towards the plain, their contours softening, jagged rock giving way to rolling green meadows. A two-man break was allowed to go after 30 kilometres and the race settled into a rhythm that mirrored the terrain.

'How are you doing, mate?' 'Me? Fucked already.' '*Sono stanchissimo …*' '*Muy cansado, tío …*' '*Très fatigué.*'

We'd been going an hour and I'd already overheard ten different versions of the same conversation, in as many languages as I could understand. The fact that guys were chatting at all was telling – and rare. Once upon a time in a Tour you'd get ten days like this, when a little group could jump away without too much opposition and over the next three or four hours the peloton would slowly but inexorably ramp up the pace and reel them in. 'TV breaks' they'd get called, pejoratively – and they'd almost died out. Nowadays everyone was either kicking the shit out of each other or on their knees, just trying to recover. Mainly the former. This stage felt like a comforting throwback.

It was tempting to savour these rare moments of relative respite but, instead, I tended to buckle down harder, become even more focused. Get even lower on the bike, more aero. I'd had a mini-epiphany in this regard early in my career in the 2009 Milan–Sanremo. The longest major one-day race in pro cycling, Sanremo is also, notoriously, the least eventful for the first four hours of racing. This one was my first edition, and I can remember being struck by how relaxed two older British riders, Jez Hunt and David Millar, had seemed as they nattered away in the first 100 kilometres of the race. Nothing wrong with old mates catching up in the bunch when the race was still easy – but Dave and Jez were in wind, doing more watts than I was tucked behind my team-mates, in my drop handlebars. Long story short, I'd win the race – my first and only monument – and the first couple of hours had been as important as the last 200 metres that some pundits still described, in 2024, as the most impressive and memorable of my career.

Only 50 kilometres to go. Gap now down to less than a minute, so no alarm there. Clouds overhead starting to darken. Can see rain in the distance and now … fuck's sake, here it comes. No time to go back for a jacket now. Hope it's a shower. Stay focused, keep fuelling. Ten kilometres to the climb, the important one, so we move towards the front for the first time, onto the shoulder of Lidl and Alpecin. I hear Renshaw on the radio: 'Harold, if you copy, please go to the front and start participating in the front so we can take good position as a team.'

Just as we'd discussed in the morning. Five kilometres from the foot of the climb, suddenly, there was Tejada. He'd ride the whole climb as though I had him on remote control, at exactly the pace we'd talked about in the morning – hard enough not to give anyone ideas, but also not so hard that I started slipping. He accelerated over the summit as teams jostled to position their leaders for the descent. The rain still fell, glazing the road, fraying nerves. Harold 'lasted' ten more kilometres. Then, with 18 kilometres to go, the Kazakhs, Fedorov and Lutsenko, powered up the right-hand side and onto the front. For the next 10 kilometres we didn't wobble, didn't waver, hugging the right curb at 55 kilometres per hour.

Eight to go. Roundabout, exit to the right and road narrows. Boys, keep right – just like we said this morning. On the right we're taking the wind but on the left there'll be more stress, more bodies. So we stay right. Out of the roundabout. We've lost Luts. Lost a few positions. For a few hundred metres Mørky and I also get separated from Ballerini and Cees. First time I've left Cees's back wheel for 50 kilometres. No stress. UAE are drilling it, then Visma … then Lotto. Five to go. Suddenly I'm on Mørky and Ballero. All good.

I hear Renshaw on the radio: 'Cav, think of Astrid! Bibidee bobbidee boo … Bibidee bobbidee boo …'

The image came, the pain faded. I mean, I don't know how long it worked, but for at least a second or two 1,000 watts felt like 100. Not that there's a lot of time in those moments for distraction. You're processing at terabytes per second, much faster than your consciousness can register sights and sounds. Chess on wheels, I called it once, but chess at warp speed is what I should have said.

Three kilometres to go and we hit the next roundabout. Again, first exit to the right, road narrows. I'm on Cees and Ballero, and Mørky's on me. Boom. I glance down at my bars and the numbers on my digital display. 58kph, 59kph, 62kph. Here we come …

I'd be asked later whether I ever practised visualising the moment. 'The moment' of course referring to the grail, the quest, the thing that had become a dream, my obsession, but also somehow the bane of my life. The R-word which made me bridle because, as I had been pointing out for four years, I had the fucking record. In answer to the question, I'd often frown as though I'd just been asked if bikes have wheels.

Of course I'd visualised. I visualised everything, always had. I think the same could be said for most athletes, and certainly the most successful ones. I hadn't needed David Spindler to teach me this: throughout my life, ever since I was an eight-year-old kid buzzing around the NSC track in Douglas in a Leeds football shirt, I'd been running simulations in my head, playing out every scenario as though in some internal video game I could never switch off. In my pro career, these daydreams simply became strategies to execute. Today's had been laid out on our team bus a few hours earlier. Now all I, all we were doing was retrofitting that plan to the real world, the actual tarmac under our tyres.

Two to go. Lotto take it up. Perfect. We're right behind them, in the slot … I've got Ballero, Cees … but Mørky can't get to us. Fuck. Lotto are coming apart now – they've gone too soon. Ballero's in the wind, it's too early, too early … but there's someone coming on the inside – the green jersey, Jonas Abrahamsen. Ballero jumps on him and we're back in business.

I glance up. Red kite. I glance down. Red kite tattooed on my forearm. Last kilometre. All in. It's now.

I'd never been the same bike rider since my illness. There, I've said it. Just don't ask me to explain why. I've had better numbers in training and races, I've felt fitter than I ever did earlier in my career, but, equally, no one will ever be able to persuade me that after 2017 I could sprint like I did at Sanremo in 2009, or at Aubenas in the Tour de France that same year. Those and a handful of other days stand out as my benchmarks. For years they also became the hammer I used on myself, ammunition for my inner critic. Why couldn't I recreate that? What had changed irrevocably? What was I doing wrong?

I would never compare myself with the great Eddy Merckx – except he happened to be the rider with whom I shared the … 'R-word'. We also shared something else: he spent the second half of his career saying similar things – that there was an inflection point in his career, after which he was never the same. For Merckx it had been a crash on an outdoor track in Blois, France, a few weeks after he'd won his first Tour. He was only 24. He continued to dominate, but insisted that something in his body or mind – probably both – felt different and, well, inferior from that day forward.

I was 31 when I was first diagnosed with Epstein–Barr in 2017. It pretty much wiped out my next four years, and clearly in that time cycling also changed. The sport was going in one direction – getting faster – while my age curve suggested that I should be regressing. Nonetheless, in 2021, I still came back and won sprints at the Tour. I was quicker, more powerful, better – the numbers said so – and yet somehow I was still reaching, straining for a sensation that I couldn't get back.

A weightlessness or liquidity. The pedals I couldn't feel. The bike melting. Everything floating, flowing like music.

With 700 metres to go I'm still on Cees … but Mørky's behind and not getting back; 650 and an Israel guy takes

Cees's wheel: Pascal Ackermann. He'll go early, Ackermann always goes early ... but he veers left and it's a choice between him and Philipsen. I go right, Philipsen, but Phil Bauhaus also wants the wheel and I have to splay my elbows, make myself bigger. *It's my wheel, you're not having it ...* Fuck's sake, Bauhaus is rigid on the bike; he ricochets off me.

At 400 it's me on Philipsen – best sprinter in last year's Tour, best team, best lead-out man with Van der Poel – but now Van der Poel's winding it up and Ackermann's on my left and I'm fucking going back with him because Ackermann always goes early.

Now 300 and Ackermann's kicked, he's gone and I've shifted left around the Lidl rider to get myself back on Ackermann's wheel. I see the 250 sign and the road's bending right, it's open road in front of Ackermann and now's the fucking time: it's now, it's me, it's the bike, 200 metres of road and a white line.

People want to hear you were in howling agony but there was none. In the last kilometre of a bike race, when I'm sprinting for a line, there's a numbness or anaesthesia that defies everything that's come before. In 2024 I wasn't the bike rider I'd been ... but one thing hadn't changed: at 1,200 watts and 180 heart beats a minute the pain receptors that had been ablaze until a few seconds earlier went offline. It didn't make sense, just as seeing my peak power numbers would have confused a lot of armchair experts. How could a rider who rarely hit 1,400 watts be beating guys who regularly produced 1,800? That, in reality, shouldn't have been much of a mystery: my 1,200 watts for 10 or more seconds would easily beat the 1,800 spike followed by the dip to 1,000 of some of my more obviously talented rivals. I'd said it many times: sprinting isn't about being fast, it's about staying fast when everyone else is tired.

100 metres.

Once you've kicked and that line's coming it can feel as though you don't need eyes. You feel riders coming, hear their distinctive noise, sense their aura, their breath and shadow. The anxiety propels you forward, because they're hunting you down: it's flight or fight. You're looking down, willing the finish line to come, almost begging, trying to kick again.

But here, now, I felt nothing. No one. Not even that flutter of anxiety suggesting they were close.

50 metres.

Faster than I could believe, sooner than I could hope, I saw the sponsor's logo painted on the tarmac under my wheels.

Then the white line.

It was done. It was over.

• • •

Pure euphoria is a great feeling but I could make a case for relief being much more satisfying. In the days that followed I'd talk a lot about a weight being lifted from my shoulders but I probably didn't or couldn't express how physical, how visceral and how instant that feeling had been. Immediately, I felt a lightness. My stomach unknotting. Cool air flowing into my lungs. As though the finish line had been a doorway to another life.

The first person I saw and embraced was the team press officer, Vitaly. I wanted to see the lads, the boys, but other bodies and faces immediately converged. Cameramen, the anti-doping chaperone and then riders from other teams: some career-long mates like Geraint, others I barely knew, had never said a word to. Faces I'd only ever seen straining and grimacing and hardly recognised. A similar thing had happened in Turkey in 2021 when I'd won for the first time in three years. I'd received plenty of admiration over the years, but real affection looked and tasted different.

Finally I spotted Cees and grabbed him, then Mørky, who was thrilled but also, I could tell, disappointed that it hadn't been a textbook lead-out. It wasn't the time or place to say it but I can now: him sticking with me and stuffing ice down my neck on stage one had contributed more to what had just happened than anything he would ordinarily have done in the last 500 metres of any stage. But Mørky's a proud guy: he wanted to do a perfect job. Harold appeared in my eyeline, then Fedorov, Ballero, Lutsenko … All any of us could say was, 'We did it. We fucking did it.'

Then the family: first Finn, who'd got a job on the Tour working as a photographer, followed by the tribe – Casper, Delilah, little Frey and of course Peta, with Astrid in her arms.

Bibidee bobbidee boo … Bibidee bobbidee boo.

The 2021 Tour wins had been memorable also because they were the first time that Casper had seen me win. I'd got him his first bike without stabilisers a few months earlier … and, the same day, I'd gone to fetch Frey from the kitchen, come back and Casper was already bombing around the driveway. He was two and a half. So him being there in 2021 was special. This left Astrid as the only one who hadn't stood with me on a Tour de France podium. Rectifying that now, just like the win itself, felt like finally being able to tie a neat bow on the top of my career.

The rest was a familiar process: anti-doping, the flash interview, the mixed-zone interviews, the press conference. I'd done it exactly … 34 times before and not too much had changed in 16 years. The Tour is a juggernaut that doesn't slow, stop or deviate for anyone or anything, and certainly not for me. The protocol is to be respected … and on this day it stretched long into the early evening.

As always, I wanted only one thing: to get back to the bus and enjoy it with the lads. When I finally got there, what struck me most – and what I still remember today – is how every smile radiated the same joy. Every last person on that bus was sharing the same emotion. Unanimous and uniform. Everyone had their own ways of expressing it – Vasi crying like Niagara Falls, howling in ecstasy, the greatest Greek dramatist of our times – but the sentiment was across the board.

My final footnote to the story of that day, maybe the defining day of my career, is a guilty confession: I didn't open my phone, didn't look at the thousands of messages of congratulations. A year later I'm still apologising to people for not replying to their texts at the time. It's the same on birthdays: the attention overwhelms me. I panic. I don't pretend to fully understand but suspect there's a piece of me that can still feel unworthy, unsafe, a recognition that with every pedestal comes a precipice. I'm haunted by a kind of superstition or fear of tempting fate – a sense that whenever good things have happened to me, inevitably, they've been followed by something negative. I think that night and in the days that followed, in particular, there was a desire to climb down from the pedestal where I'd put myself and others had elevated me for the last decade and a half. Maybe that, more than anything else, explained the relief when I crossed the line; the knowledge that I was leaving that rarefied air, that I wouldn't experience the same highs, but that life would feel safer closer to ground level.

It was over. And that suited me just fine.

Oh, and I lied about the messages. I did open one. It was from Vasi. Having mastered the art of tragedy and satire, he'd apparently turned his hand to parody.

The following, I'm assuming, was supposed to be read in the voice of Markos Cavendishopoulos:

I'm twisted.
I feel sick

Something's wrong with my body
It's so windy over here
It's fucken windy at this fucken mountain
I stop the effort

He signed off: 'Would I change anything if I could go back in time? NO! Thanks for this journey mate! We fucken did it!!!!!!!!!!!'

The reply is still in my drafts: 'Vasi, it's "fucking", not "fucken". Love you too.'

EPILOGUE

t's become a truism in elite sport that dealing with failure is straightforward – it's dealing with success that you have to learn. I'd been confronted with this in the early years of my career and now, potentially, would have to face a different version of the same problem. What can fill a void where until a moment earlier an all-consuming passion burned? Or as the Olympic swimmer Michael Phelps once put it,

> If your whole life was about building up to one race, one performance, or one event, how does that sustain everything that comes afterward? ... Eventually, for me at least, there was one question that hit me like a ton of bricks: Who was I outside of the swimming pool?

Other sporting legends have talked about 'anti-climax' or 'deflation', of finding out that the 'arrival fallacy' is just that – the mistaken idea that life will be complete just as soon as an ambition is fulfilled. I'll be honest and say that I didn't feel any of that. Yes, over the remaining two and a half weeks of the Tour, a light did go out ... but I'd be lying if I said this was the cause of great existential angst. The relief remained. A sweet surrender to passing time and the ending of a chapter.

There was frustration, too, but it was mundane, you might even say petty. 'Petty' was certainly the word I would use for what set it off. The very next day and stage six from Mâcon to Dijon *should* have presented an opportunity for win number 36. I was motivated, the boys seemed ready, and now even the pundits were predicting that, as it had in other years, my first stage win would open the floodgates. I'd won stage five with such aplomb – and such a margin – that it was suddenly hard to imagine who could stop me.

I'd told the lads in the bus that we needed to stay vigilant, because the wind could split the race. I'd noticed a few of them looking a little bit too relaxed early in the stage, then, sure enough, we hit a section of narrow roads snaking through vineyards and suddenly Visma–Lease a Bike ripped the peloton apart. I was our only guy in the front split, but not for long: another puncture and, with the team cars behind the last group or echelon on the road, I could only stand there and wait for help to arrive. When it did, a TV cameraman wanted to capture the moment, but in doing so completely blocked the road. I asked him politely to move … then a little less politely. By the time I could get going again a commissaire had appeared to tell me that the team cars wouldn't be allowed to pass me and that I therefore couldn't ride through the convoy and back to the peloton. Basically I was now 'barraged' or getting the same treatment as someone who had been dropped. To get back to the peloton – bridge around a kilometre of clear air between me and them – I'd need a miracle.

My 'conversation' with the commissaire continued as I hammered on the pedals. My team-mates had dropped back to help and, over the next ten kilometres, the pace at the front slowed to the extent that we could rejoin the bunch. But I was still fuming. And, that night, I'd still somehow get fined 200 Swiss francs and hit with a 40-second penalty for drafting behind my team car. This when, had the TV motorbike not blocked the road, I'd have been in the team cars and sheltered the whole time.

I still had a couple of hours to compose myself for the sprint, but somehow the whole thing had thrown me. We, especially I, made a hash of the finale and I crossed the line nineteenth. Nowhere. Now I was rushing to get back to the bus not to celebrate but to apologise.

The next morning I'd even speak to the boss of France Télévisions to explain how and why his camera bikes needed to stay a little bit further out of the way. The whole incident had left me demoralised, as though I didn't know what I could and couldn't do any more. I'd encountered the same frustrations before, to be sure, but the difference now was that, having got to 35 stage wins, the war felt over – with the record, my rivals, myself and, yes, even certain commissaires and their fickle interpretation of the rules. I still desperately wanted to win stages but I didn't need to. As much as my conscious mind couldn't admit that to itself, on a deeper, cellular level, I think I felt it. I was slowly checking out. The light was starting to flicker, dim and fade.

I was never going to down tools. I also still believed I could win. But something had definitely shifted. As with the commissaires on stage six, the little annoyances seemed pettier than ever – and like further vindication for my decision to get out. In the finale on stage eight, I bickered with one of Biniam Girmay's domestiques, Laurenz Rex, and remember thinking that it was all too dangerous and that everyone needed to chill the fuck out. There, I got on the radio and told Cees to sprint but I was pulling the pin. Then, two days later, we had the gravel stage through Champagne country – supposedly a throwback to cycling's 'glory days' of unpaved roads, only there was nothing glorious about the way some of the present generation went about things. One of the oldest, until recently least contentious unwritten rules in cycling dictates that when the leader of a stage race, and particularly the Tour de France, stops for a 'nature break', no one attacks. Well, on this day that rule had clearly been forgotten or tossed out, because when Pogačar stopped at a 'quiet' moment in the first hour or so of the race, off riders went down the road. No fucking mercy – not even for Tadej Pogačar. At moments like this, and certainly on that day, I found myself thinking that I still loved professional cycling but I didn't recognise it any more. No one wants to become that grumpy old man waxing nostalgic about his halcyon days and lamenting the youth of today, yet increasingly that's who I was turning into. Clearly, just like at the Giro in 2023, I could feel my spirit floating off towards the cycling afterlife, both feet still clipped into the pedals but one of them metaphorically already in the grave.

These were mostly vague stirrings in my subconscious for a few days, but stage 12 to Villeneuve-sur-Lot was the fire extinguisher to whatever flame was still alive. The day had started badly with Mørky testing positive for Covid and having to leave the Tour. That aside, there was nothing wrong with my motivation at the start, or my legs. The stage was long and the terrain deceptively undulating – punitive enough to sift out a lot of sprinters before we even approached the finale. Even during the sprint, though, I felt strange, as though something was holding me back. The hyper-focus that I'd usually be able to access in the closing kilometres – that clarity in the chaos – just wasn't there. I committed to the extent that I finished sixth having just ran out of road, but instincts, my reflexes, maybe even my will, felt muffled or muted. As though my handbrake was never fully released.

It was the aftermath, though, that really put out my fire. Shortly after the finish we were informed that the commissaires had reviewed the sprint and decided that I was guilty of a 'deviation from the chosen line that obstructs or endangers another rider or irregular sprint'. In short, in their view, I had swung abruptly left with around 150 metres to go and this had put the other sprinters, and particularly the Cofidis rider Bryan Coquard in peril. They had relegated me to last place in my group of riders.

Once again, I was at a loss. I'd moved left because there was nowhere else I could go to avoid crashing myself and bringing down other riders. The Arkéa lead-out man Dan McLay had created the hazard by stopping his effort in the middle of the road and then dropping back through the middle of the pack like a rock through a mineshaft. If I hadn't swerved, I'd have ploughed into the back of him.

At the start the next morning I tried to make my case to the commissaires. I said I'd basically had three options: go right and force other riders into the barriers; ride into the back of Dan McLay because there was no time to brake; or, three, do what I'd done – take evasive action. They pretty much just shrugged. Rules were rules. Common sense or me having done the safest thing for all concerned was … pffff, for the birds.

The Tour route was so backloaded that there were only two potential sprints left: one the following day in Pau and the other in Nîmes on stage 16. If I already felt a fraction less hungry and less dialled in before, now I sensed myself sliding further off my game. The problem was practical as much as emotional: I simply didn't understand what was and what wasn't permitted any more. This created a sort of paralysis. You introduce doubt and hesitation into a sprinter's mind and you saw off his legs. I felt bad for the boys because they were still committing, still performing, sacrificing their race for mine. But I just couldn't push all my chips forward.

It was also the case that, as we moved towards the Pyrenees, my priorities had switched. One obsession was still eating at me – and that was finishing the Tour in Nice. I had spent the last five years trying to ensure that my career didn't end with a whimper, on a bum note. Winning my thirty-fifth stage had been historic, the perfect fairy tale – but I had a bit to go before the 'happily ever after'. The prospect of now getting eliminated in the Pyrenees or Alps still terrorised me. A Cinderella story where the glass slippers fitted perfectly but shattered just before she reached the altar had limited appeal.

Stage 15 to Plateau de Beille in the Pyrenees had always looked the most problematic. It started with three monster climbs in the first 70 kilometres then finished with an even tougher, higher trifecta. I was dropped on the first climb of the day, the Peyresourde, but immediately the guys gathered around: Ballerini, Cees, Lutsenko. The middle section of the stage was one long grind through a valley. Here Lutsenko, in particular, bored through the headwind like a power drill while I sheltered on his wheel. Every watt I saved could be the difference between me making the time cut or not. We weren't the only ones in the same predicament – and some things I saw beggared belief: riders falling behind, way behind us, then miraculously reappearing with their team cars a few kilometres up the road;

guys cooking themselves to stay ahead of us on climbs then blowing up.

At the bottom of the final climb we knew that it'd be tight, but we were also on pace with the plan that Vasi had drawn up. It was now just a case of unloading all the power I had left. We finally made it two minutes before the drawbridge went up. I'd come over the line swinging and swaying, completely empty. A different sort of relief this time – and it was soon tempered by the usual catcalls from social media. A certain corner of the Internet couldn't believe I'd made it through, and were soon brandishing their own in-depth statistical analysis to substantiate their theory that I'd cheated: apparently I'd taken 'only' 13 minutes more than Tadej Pogačar to ride up the final climb. One coach from another team even approached Vasi quoting the same numbers and asking how I'd done it. Vasi simply gave him my power file. It was all there. If the guy had looked closely, and maybe compared it to his own sprinter's, he'd have seen how economically I'd ridden the whole stage, unlike his rider who we'd seen yo-yoing all day.

I shouldn't have cared or got annoyed but it did grate. I'd heard the same nonsense since the start of my career. There'd been no evolution in some of the thought processes, no thought that maybe they should try to understand how I rode before they defaulted to scorn or suspicion. These guys had had nine months after a Tour route was unveiled to plan like we had for this one. But their egos wouldn't allow them to contemplate things going south, it becoming a fight to survive; they had no contingency plans. I saw it year after year, from riders earning millions. They'd rather just get off their bikes and abandon. And then critique and question someone who was able to deal with the adversity because they'd done the disaster planning months in advance.

Anyway, that was for them to figure out. I had less than a week to go, one more mountain range. Probably only three more days that could potentially bring down the guillotine. The summit finish at Isola 2000 looked the most daunting. The main climb on the route, the Cime de la Bonette, was the highest main road in France. I also had horrible memories of Isola from 2019, when I'd gone up there to prepare for the Tour, only for Dimension Data not to select me. There was another bad omen: an almost identical stage to the same alpine resort in the 1993 Tour de France had been the last of the two-time Tour champion Laurent Fignon's career.

It turned out to be much less of an ordeal than Plateau de Beille. On the final climb to Isola 2000, I even went too fast and pissed off Cees and Ballero. 'What the fuck are you doing?' they screamed at one point. For most of the Tour it had been me shouting the same thing at Ballero. I just wanted it over with, so had disregarded Vasi's schedule. That whole place and climb lurked in my nightmares.

The next day, the final mountain stage, turned out to be a much less harrowing experience. I knew every climb, had done them all countless times in training with Geraint and Luke Rowe. I also had diamonds in my legs – I was fucking flying. On the first climb to the Col de Braus, I had to sit up and actually wait for the gruppetto. Soon we were so far ahead of schedule that any concern about missing the time cut evaporated and I could actually enjoy the ride. Savour it, with Cees and Ballero at my side. These were my last ever mountains as a pro bike rider. It was like breaking bread with an old enemy, the climbs themselves rolling over and conceding defeat. I could cherish every metre – the fans, the company of my team-mates, even the views of the surrounding mountains and some of the memories. I've mentioned Laurent Fignon's last day as a Tour rider in 1993. He described a similar experience on what he'd already decided would be his final climb, in his case the Bonette – putting his hands on the top of his handlebars and letting his mind wander; of it being a 'poetic distillation' of his career, a moment of 'total harmony'.

My own, almost spiritual last ascent was to the finish line of the Col de la Couillole. Now we rode at a comfortable pace not to save energy for the time trial but simply to drink in the scene and atmosphere. We let the gruppetto peel away from and ahead of us, making the moment even more intimate. It became even more special when three kilometres from the line, I spotted a jersey the same turquoise shade as our own among the fans on one side of the road. Harold Tejada, the best climber in our team, had stopped – literally got off his bike and was standing, waiting – so that he could ride the last three kilometres with us. The next few minutes were some of the most emotional I'd ever experienced as a bike rider. Around 1,500 metres from the line, tears started welling and then wouldn't stop. Our Tour would be remembered for my thirty-fifth stage win, but we all knew that the most meaningful moments for us had come in adversity. They'd be the times we'd reminisce about in 30 years, what connected our group of international misfits riding in Kazakh colours for life.

More tears came as I rounded the last corner. In them was mainly pride at knowing that we would accomplish what we'd set out to do: finish the Tour. I was reaching the end of a longer journey – but I'd get to celebrate and process that in the time trial the following day. I didn't know too much at this point about the life that lay ahead. I was just sure that, from the one I was leaving behind, the kind of comradeship that I'd experienced over the previous three weeks was what I would miss the most.

. . .

Cinderella had finished her fairytale in the glass slippers – they remained sparklingly intact – and I'd have my equivalent. Years earlier, I'd been introduced to the artist Damien Hirst by a mutual friend. For my final Tour, Damien had agreed to decorate a pair of my racing shoes with one of his famous butterfly patterns – and it was wearing those that I'd finish my career in Nice.

Damien's butterflies symbolised beauty and love but also, mainly, the fragility of life and resurrection. I'm sure Vasi would tell you that the ancient Greeks were the first to make the association between butterflies and the soul. They had the same word for both, psyche, and a goddess of the soul with that name.

I'd started to get interested in art during the Covid lockdown. I wasn't and still wouldn't profess to be a great expert. I'm also less interested in the meaning of artworks than their aesthetics. Nonetheless, the butterflies and resurrection motif seemed highly fitting. My career had been pronounced and sometimes even felt dead on more than one occasion. Sometimes it had seemed as though I was going through the same cycle of life every season: of being written off, dismissed, declared extinct, only to re-emerge and reinvent myself. But the years between 2017 and 2021 had been the redemption arc that defined me, my deepest crisis followed by my miraculous rebirth. The three years since then had been their own reincarnation story – but now an even more fundamental transformation awaited. I wasn't afraid but wasn't naive, either: this, too, would be difficult. It was a common trope but also a well-documented truth among retired riders that it took three years, on average, to adjust to 'civilian' life. That estimate also referred to an era before long training camps and periods away from home, when the transition was less stark. Friends warned that it'd be especially difficult for me. My identity had been built on my exalted status in a self-contained, insular world which I was now exiting. I also had a big family and financial pressures. Business ideas that lacked clarity. Lingering mental health issues that might still flare. I liked to think that I understood and was ready for all of this. But I was under no illusions about it being easy, of coasting towards some honeyed existence on a sun lounger.

Damien's art had resonated with me for another reason. He was divisive – not only in the sense that his work wasn't universally liked, but also, above all, because there were those who wouldn't accept that he was even an artist. That very debate, to me, proved his credentials instantly: an artist is someone whose work provokes debate. In this I could identify, because if there was one thing that I'd been in my career, as well as successful, it was divisive. Loved and admired by many, fucking detested by others. No more a 'proper' rider than Damien was a real artist – 'only' a sprinter. Brash, narky and outspoken, particularly early in my career, until I got so fed up of my words and thoughts being twisted or misunderstood that I hardly ever did interviews away from races. It wasn't all the media's fault: I divided opinion, too, because I had and still have a chip on my shoulder the size of the Grand Canyon. Maybe people picked at and exacerbated it, but there were no excuses: sometimes I behaved like a … well, I won't say. It took living with Peta and for her to show me why I was being an idiot to understand. But, yes, there was no doubt I was divisive and remained that throughout my career. How could I not be with my Chip, and with my inability to see that not everyone's brain worked the same way as mine? Someone with those characteristics is destined to polarise an audience. It cost me a lot of energy and caused me great anguish over the years ... but I couldn't lobotomise whole parts of myself. Peta's influence and watching the kids mirror certain behaviours just taught me that wisdom isn't always about being right – it's also about being empathetic and knowing how to deliver my message.

Mentally, through my various struggles, there was no doubt that I'd become resilient, but I was also thankful to be stepping away with my physical health intact. There was relief for me – and certainly for Peta – in knowing that the descent off the Col de la Colmiane on stage 20 was the last time I'd have to bomb down a mountain road at speeds pushing 100 kilometres per hour in a race. A year earlier, just before the Tour, my old team-mate from Dimension Data, the Swiss rider Gino Mäder, had fallen to his death on the road off the Albulapass in the Tour de Suisse. Gino was a lovely lad – deeply intelligent and thoughtful, always upbeat, with a smile that could light up a team bus. His death had been not only a tragedy but a chilling reminder to the rest of us. Numerous times in my career, after the fact, I'd thought to myself that I'd taken too many risks and that it had to be the last time. Then, though, you'd find yourself in a race situation that felt as though it demanded the same recklessness and you'd do it again ... Because reckless is what it was at times, particularly on certain descents in the Tour de France, with Bernie Eisel and I racing to make the time cut. You're rubbing up against the limits of gravity and physics, on a rubber razor's edge, wearing nothing but the thinnest layer of Lycra, telling yourself you're in control, but at the mercy of the tiniest pothole or piece of debris. This in a peloton where no inch is given – and certainly not the metre or two that everyone left to the rider in front on descents at the start of my career, just to be safe. This, of course – safety and the disregard riders now showed for each other in the bunch – was another sore subject, and another facet of 'modern cycling' that I wouldn't miss.

Towards the end of 2024 I was invited to participate in an online seminar with many of the top sprinters in the sport, male and female, to discuss what could be done to make racing less dangerous. That threw up some interesting discussion points but also viewpoints that left me scratching my head. I'd need a whole other book to deliver all of my thoughts on the matter, so here I'll limit myself to just one recommendation: that every rider aspiring to turn professional be required to take and pass both a theory and practical test before obtaining their licence. I don't want to discredit anyone for a lack of experience, but it stands to reason that super-talented athletes plucked from other sports or online racing may have missed key phases in their education. Instead of dropping them into the pro peloton and seeing if they sink, swim or drown someone else with them, why not just give them a little help?

In some ways the direction of travel worried me, but there was also no denying that, in other respects, it was a more salubrious environment than the one in which I'd arrived when I joined T-Mobile in 2007. Then, the reputation of the sport was described by World Anti-Doping Agency president Dick Pound as 'in the toilet'. Pound was referring to the regular drumbeat of doping scandals that had become the sport's signature song. The 2006 Tour de France was ruined before it even started, the two pre-race favourites getting booted out on the eve of the race. I made my debut in the next edition, which was no less scandal-marred, then my four stage wins in 2008 came against the inescapable backdrop of more positive tests, more suspicions, more talk of cycling having hit rock bottom. Just before that 2007 Tour, the governing body, the UCI, had invited me to their headquarters in Switzerland to become the first signatory of a new 'anti-doping' charter. Their goal was to upend the sport's culture and transform it from one which encouraged and protected dopers to one in which they were no longer tolerated.

At the time a lot of people thought cycling was a lost cause. But over the next few years I did see that culture change, not because of that UCI charter or any other single measure or edict, but rather a general recognition that it couldn't go on. Riders who had raced and, yes, themselves cheated in those dark times also became key agents of change. They could see from their own experience that a sport where you had to dope to win or even just keep up was one in which everybody lost. I'd never needed reminding of that message – but guys like Rolf Aldag, who fessed up about his own doping in 2007, made sure that I heard and understood it anyway.

Attitudes had shifted, testing methodologies and frequency improved, and now, in 2024, I was departing a sport in which doping had faded from the agenda. Positive tests and police investigations seemed to have become a thing of the past. Sometimes I'd get asked: was that because no one doped or because no one got caught? I wouldn't know the answer … but could only say honestly that my suspicion was almost never aroused. Or, when it was, the guy had almost always been caught in the weeks or months that followed. The last example I could think of was an Italian rider called Andrea Piccolo. He seemed a bit of an unconventional, flamboyant character, and he'd followed a bit of a meandering path to the WorldTour, but it wasn't either of those things that set my alarm bells ringing. At Tour Colombia in 2024, something just seemed 'off' with the way he was climbing, in particular. A few of the guys in the team mentioned it. After a while you develop an eye for these things. And, well, in this case my – our – intuition was right. Weeks later Piccolo got sacked by his team.

So I was leaving an undeniably healthier sport than the one that had greeted me in 2007. The litmus test often applied was – 'Would you be happy for your kids to follow your path?' This was a question I'd had to contemplate, with Casper's passion burning so bright. It hasn't been easy for any of our kids in their various sporting endeavours as the children of a famous sporting father. Classmates or even their parents would say things ... Once Finn went to watch Delilah play netball and overheard two of the dads talking. 'That's Mark Cavendish's daughter,' one of them said, 'but of course he's never here. Too busy chasing the money ...' Finn, bless him, interrupted to tell them that he was Delilah's brother and, since they were clearly interested, Mark was racing today but there was always someone watching Delilah's games – be it Mark, Peta or another family member. Naturally, Casper will get plenty of this if he decides to pursue cycling. I didn't come from a cycling dynasty – a cycling anything – but my parents were great in the sense that they supported my passion, were there if I needed them, but didn't meddle or apply unnecessary pressure. I could have nice kit ... but I had to save up and buy it, so that I'd learn to value it. Obviously it's a bit different for Casper, but I try to abide by some of the same principles. He already races because he's desperate to race, even though I think he's too young. But he rides an entry-level, off-the-peg bike, with kids that turn up on bikes that cost thousands, don't fit them, and are tricked out with all sorts of kit they don't need. My only rule, whether it's his cycling or Delilah's netball, is that if they've chosen to participate, they commit. The only times I've got upset with them were when they wanted to give up because they weren't winning, or didn't get picked for a team. I don't ever intend to force the morals of my sporting career down my kids' necks … but if there is one takeaway, surely, it's that you don't quit.

Whether assimilating or inheriting that will be enough to bring Casper a career in professional cycling – and whether he'll even want that – of course remains to be seen. It could well be that other life lessons I have to impart will be well beyond their date of utility then. No doubt, like all embarrassing dads, I'll still try. Warn him never to trust a handshake – something I learned the hard way. Explain that there are good people in professional cycling but also plenty of snakes. Make sure he remembers what brought him there in the first place, just like it did me – a love of cycling that will be tested but will always endure.

. . .

A final confession: I was delighted that the Tour de France 2024 would not finish on the Champs-Elysées. The most famous avenue in the world, the most beautiful boulevard, scene of my most iconic sprints … it was otherwise engaged with the Olympics and that suited me just fine. In a normal year, in addition to the stress and anticipation of the inevitable sprint even in the hours and days beforehand, there was always the chance that an otherwise successful Tour could end badly, with a bitter taste. I'd seen that in 2021. Now, not only was there no final showdown on the horizon, I would also be riding, basking and saying farewell alone, in a time trial, on the stunning roads leading to a city that I loved,

Nice. A month later, incidentally, I'd be back there receiving the city's highest honour, the Aigla Nissarda, and honorary citizenship, from the mayor, my friend Christian Estrosi.

Not many days in my career had flirted with perfection but the last one came close. I can remember just one thing that didn't go according to plan: our radios not working, meaning I didn't hear Casper screaming encouragement from the team car, or Mark Renshaw's emotional speech as I rode towards the finish line. Everything else about the day had been magical. It started with a beautiful ceremony to thank me for my contribution to the Tour – when really it was me who wanted to thank them for giving me a career, an identity, a *raison d'être*. I then rolled down the start ramp in Monaco and into a 33-kilometre-long corridor of noise on familiar roads, suspended above one of the world's most gorgeous coastlines. Again, I tried to wrap myself in every cheer, mentally bottle and appreciate every smile. The last climb of my life would be one I'd done many times – the Col d'Èze. I climbed it as though crowd-surfing to the summit, glorying in every pedal rev.

I was crying again by the time I reached the Promenade des Anglais and the closing metres. Maybe 50 metres from the finish line, through my happy tears, I also saw a face that I immediately recognised: the legendary British commentator Phil Liggett. Later I rewatched the American network NBC's broadcast and heard Phil do something highly unusual: tell the viewers that he was leaving the commentary box for a second because he wanted to see me finish my Tour de France career. Phil had covered the Tour for five decades. To think that he would grant me that honour was incredibly humbling.

I crossed the line and rode into the embrace of Peta and the kids. They had nearly not made it to Nice. They – we – hadn't wanted to jinx it all by booking accommodation in Nice more than three or four days before I arrived … and when we finally started looking there was nothing left. It was in situations like this that you saw the value of real friends and long-term partners, in this case the watchmaker Richard Mille. I'd called one of my contacts there and they'd said not to worry. They ended up booking and insisting on paying for rooms in a Nice institution, Le Negresco.

There was something poetic even about that. The hotel had appeared in countless films and music videos, one of which could have doubled as my goodbye speech. The singer was another honorary citizen of Nice, Elton John, and the song's chorus, 'I'm still standing, better than I ever did. Lookin' like a true survivor …'

PICTURE CREDITS

Steve Walsh / PA Images / Alamy Stock Photo
(Image 2)

Sprint Cycling Agency
(Image 6)

MARCO BERTORELLO / Contributor / Getty Images
(Image 18)

Other images courtesy of Mark Cavendish
and Vasilis Anastopoulos.